Cover: Casa Florencia, staircase. *Historical Society of Palm Beach County.*

Back Cover: Casa Florencia, loggia. *Historical Society of Palm Beach County.*

PALM BEACH

A GREATER GRANDEUR

AUGUSTUS MAYHEW

For my mother

Lucille Sanderson Mayhew

Published by East Side Press   Book Design by Patrizia Sceppa

Copyright © 2016 by Augustus Mayhew

CONTENTS

Above. Ceilito Lindo, façade. Marion Sims Wyeth, architect. *Historical Society of Palm Beach County.*

INTRODUCTION

Palm Beach's transformation from an idyllic seasonal refuge and international resort to a posh year-round residential enclave makes for a fascinating architectural history as well as an enlightening account of the customs observed by the nation's wealthiest families, industrial titans and Wall Street tycoons. Ever since Henry Flagler's Whitehall overshadowed the resort's low profile cottages, commanding the same magnitude as his colossal hotels, successive generations have come to Palm Beach and built their own Taj Mahals while indulging in most every pleasure money can buy.

During the peak of the 1920s real estate boom, as Addison Mizner blueprints delineated a ninety-room mansion, a fifty-foot drawing room and a twenty-car garage, Palm Beach cottages were supplanted by Newport-sized mansions. Just as Mar-A-Lago neared completion, its impressive splendor heralded as the quintessential Palm Beach folly, work had already begun on its nearby complement, Cielito Lindo, architect Marion Sims Wyeth's magnum opus. Dreamed up without Mar-A-Lago's complex extravagance, the Hispano-Moresque palace's sublime play of imaginative realism made for a more cohesive vision bound by immense sea gardens that magically conveyed the effect of floating between the sky and the ocean.

Much of the fabled resort's story has always revolved around perpetuating its fabled location between Babylon and Brigadoon. Rather than reconstruct the past from a bygone mix of recurring anecdotes and myths, these essays utilize previously untapped primary resources that offer a different perspective on the past. In several instances, they make us rethink what we thought we already knew about Palm Beach.

The Mary Fanton Roberts Papers (1880-1956) at The Smithsonian's Archives of American Art contains handwritten correspondence and telegrams from Paris Singer and family members that have not previously been considered in recounting Singer's life in New York and Palm Beach. Digitized in 2007, these archival documents clarify our understanding for the inspiration and construction of the Everglades Club. If it was not for the concentration of research materials available at Princeton University's Firestone Library Rare Books & Special Collections, Otto Kahn's significant role in the development of Palm Beach's exclusive private clubs could never be acknowledged. During the decades that the Honorable James R. Knott officiated at countless Palm Beach weddings, the noted historian, circuit court judge and former president of the Historical Society of Palm Beach County kept a detailed diary where he remarked on the ceremonies, settings and personalities at these occasions. Judge Knott's notations are an unrestrained look at the idiosyncrasies unique to Palm Beach.

While today's Palm Beach residents may not always adhere to the ideals and standards that past eras professed, they share the same quixotic search for paradise that first attracted their predecessors. For more than a century, Palm Beach has preserved its unique paradoxical attraction — an ultimate journey's end and a place to pursue a greater grandeur.

ACKNOWLEDGMENTS

Palm Beach: A Greater Grandeur is an informative collection of essays about Palm Beach's social, cultural and architectural history originally published at *The New York Social Diary, Palm Beach Daily News* and *Palm Beach Life* magazine. I am grateful to David Patrick Columbia and Jeff Hirsch at *NYSD*, Joyce Reingold, former editor and publisher of *The Palm Beach Daily News,* and Darrell Hofheinz, editor of *Palm Beach Life* magazine. I owe special thanks to John Tucker, Local and Family History Librarian at Torquay Library, for making available materials on Paris Singer and the Singer family. The vast archive found within the Otto H. Kahn Papers, Manuscript Division, Department of Rare Books and Special Collections, Princeton University Library, allowed me to record new chapters in Palm Beach's social history. For their help and guidance, I am indebted to Debi Murray, chief curator at the Historical Society of Palm Beach County, and Nick Golubov, the Historical Society's research and curatorial assistant.

Above. "The Plan of Palm Beach." Sketch, 1929. Bennett, Parsons & Frost, consulting architects. *Town of Palm Beach Collection.*

Palm Beach Florida

Most Popular Resort in the World

Hotel Royal Poinciana

Fred Sterry and H. E. Bemis, Managers

The Breakers

Leland Sterry, Manager

Eighteen=Hole Golf Course.   Deep=sea Fishing from Ocean Pier.   Surf and Pool Bathing.   Electric and Naptha Launches and Sail Boats on Lake Worth.   Finest Trails for Bicycle Chairs in the World A Southern Resort With Surf Bathing.   Equable Sunny Climate.   Superb Hotel Accommo- dations.   Finest and Most Roman- tic Scenery on Earth

"EVERYBODY   GOES   TO   PALM   BEACH"

Above. Advertisement. Palm Beach: Most Popular Resort in the World. *Palm Beach Life archive.*

1

THE ASPHALT JUNGLE
BUILDING HISTORY AT PALM BEACH

Palm Beach streets are lined with a variety of architectural styles that were determined as much by the economics of dividing ocean-to-lake estates into residential subdivisions as formulated by periodic aesthetic shifts, storms, lawsuits, and politics. Beginning with Henry Flagler's "Pay-no-matter-the-price!" acquisition of a lakefront hotel site that triggered Palm Beach's first land boom, until more than a century later, when Charles Bingham's descendants sold the last vestige of their pioneer-era Figulus estate as part of a $130 million transaction, real estate development has been the island's main attraction.

At one time, Palm Beach's allure was its secluded tropical setting interconnected by a patchwork of quays, footpaths and wheelchair trails. When oceanfront and lakeside hotels were added, the resort's golf course became its centerpiece encircled by railroad tracks. Having since shed its resort image and reinvented itself as an exclusive residential enclave, Palm Beach swapped its exotic ambiance for commonplace subdivisions, accommodating picture-book cottages and colossal mansions with imposing facades aligned on paved cul de sacs and thoroughfares. Palm Beach's residential construction industry has endured as the town's most commercial enterprise however much Worth Avenue's shops, County Road's boutiques and Royal Palm Way's phalanx of office buildings are perceived as the town's business district.

Unlike Newport's ensembles of period buildings reflecting a collective history, Palm Beach streetscapes have been fragmented and unsettled for the better part of the past century. Today, streets are as overridden by speculative construction sites, staged listings and properties owned by anonymous limited liability companies as they are lived in by actual residents. Midtown bungalows have been replaced with parking lots, townhouse rows and multi-story condominiums. Mansion styles once reserved for the Estate Section are now squeezed onto smaller sites on Everglades Island and the North End. Early on, Palm Beach established a repetitive cycle where for the most part each succeeding generation has done away with the previous era's housing styles deemed passé and obsolete. The continuous pursuit of construction and reconstruction has made the town an ultimate destination for architects, builders, construction companies, designers, and real estate agents.

From Shangri-La to Showplaces

At the outset, Palm Beach's terrain was a morass of coconut groves, pineapple fields and backyard gardens. Trails and footpaths made from packed-down tall grass and saw palmetto fronds led across marshes to bluffs overlooking the ocean. Afar, the distant Gulf Stream current; below, a broad stretch of beach blanketed with shells. Properties were advertised for sale either by Lake Trail or Jungle Trail. A January 1891 *New York Times* article described Palm Beach as the garden spot of Florida, stating "There are no roads because none are needed."

With the introduction of resort hotels and the tourist industry, the primary means for arriving and navigating the island became railway cars, a mule-drawn trolley and wheelchairs. Years after the opening of the Flagler-built hotels, Palm Beach still consisted of only a few hotels, a small number of multi-acre estates, hotels, and thirty cottages. Visitors and pioneer families shared the same appreciation for the island's uncultivated nature.

By January 1906, Henry Flagler had completed a sixty-six mile road to the south from West Palm Beach to Miami that for a distance consisted only of a trail through the woods and canebrakes. Yet, there was still no navigable road north of Palm Beach to the Ormond-Daytona Beach area where during the winter season a large influx of auto enthusiasts converged for speed racing before heading to Lake Worth's Motorboat Carnival and Regatta. They had no alternative to reach Palm Beach except to board trains for the one-hundred eighty-five mile trip to the south.

Above. The railroad brought seasonal tourists who changed Palm Beach from a remote refuge to a resort. *Library of Congress*.

Below. The Jungle Trail led sightseers through a tangle of tropical habitats to attractions such as a colossal rubber tree, an ostrich feather showroom and an alligator farm. *Library of Congress*.

Above. Located midway between today's Flagler Museum and The Society of the Four Arts, the Coconut Grove Hotel was established by Elisha N. "Cap," and Ella Dimick, The popularity of the eight-room boarding house resulted in its expansion into a fifty-room hotel charging six dollars per day for room and board. *State of Florida Archive.*

Below. By 1900 Henry Flagler's 1,000-room Hotel Royal Poinciana was considered the world's largest wood-frame building. *Library of Congress.*

In 1908 an expedition left Jacksonville to measure the three-hundred seventy-one mile extent of passable roadway to Miami while placing mileage and directional information on signboards nailed to trees. These explorers, accompanied by a surveyor and a reporter, made the trip driving a forty-horsepower Cleveland Pathfinder. They survived the five-day excursion carrying a pickaxe, spade, block and tackle, pine planks, and a camping tent for a journey where they encountered snakes, skunks and vultures. Their escapade took them on trails with grass as high as the radiator and swamps a foot deep.

That same year, four of Palm Beach's most prominent citizens — Harvey Geer, George Jonas, Elisha "Cap" Dimick, and Otto Kubin — formed the Royal Park Improvement Company, acquiring a one-hundred sixty acre ocean-to-lake parcel located south of the Royal Poinciana Hotel. This platted residential development began Palm Beach's transformation from an exclusive resort for the few to an accessible vacation home getaway for the many.

Welcome to Royal Park

The Royal Park Improvement Company dredged the lake to fill-in the marshes and bogs before it platted the parcel with building lots suitable for cottages and bungalows. The subdivision's impressive entranceway was named Royal Palm Way, patterned after Chicago's Drexel Boulevard. The streets were identified as Cocoanut and Hibiscus, for the plantings that lined them; Australian, Brazilian and Chilean, for their exotic locations. Its southern boundary was Worth Avenue, honoring William Jenkins Worth, a brigadier-general during the Second Seminole War. By 1911, a privately-owned wooden toll bridge was built connecting Royal Palm Way with West Palm Beach. While the north bridge was still only a railroad-pedestrian corridor, the Royal Park Bridge was wide enough for two vehicles to pass, allowing automobiles to drive onto the island.

During the years Royal Park was being built, other developers were inspired to survey and plat their own subdivisions. In January 1912, as George Jonas was moving into his new Royal Park home, brothers Edward R. and John Bradley, proprietors of the legendary Beach Club, platted Sunrise Avenue on the north side of Main Street in the new Floral Park subdivision. Prompted by the editorial enthusiasm of *The Tropical Sun* newspaper and the Flagler-owned *Palm Beach Daily News*, tourists were encouraged to buy property. Directly north of Royal Park and south of the Royal Poinciana Hotel, Indiana developer Oscar Jose's City Builders' Realty Company platted the Poinciana Park subdivision from the Frederick Robert and James Stillman estates. Promising no cheap structures, lot auctions lured participants as the developer advertised "One dozen solid gold watches will be given away whether you buy or not." A local editorial stated, "Palm Beach would no longer be owned by people owning large chunks who did not care to sell which created an exclusiveness that limited the island to big hotel properties and the palatial homes of the comparatively few winter residents."

The asphalt jungle

During the summer of 1912, Colonel Samuel Goodman signed a contract with the Town of Palm Beach to build an ocean road for $10,000. First called Gulf Stream Drive, the scenic road would extend north five miles from the pier at The Breakers to what was then the inlet and south eighteen miles to Delray. A retired textile manufacturer and the owner of a North End ocean-to-lake estate, Goodman was a former president of the Chestnut Hill Improvement Association, where he had directed the paving of that community's fifteen miles of roadway. Petitions were signed supporting the fifty-foot wide thoroughfare running along the ocean bluff. When completed the ocean boulevard would be not only the most picturesque road in Florida but also its twenty-three mile length from Palm Beach to Delray would make it the longest ocean boulevard in the world. *The Tropical Sun* proclaimed, "The spirit of progress and development was about to take hold, making the island accessible by automobile, allowing machines to go up and down the scenic boulevard."

With the construction of a boulevard along the ocean and the introduction of subdivisions, many of Palm Beach's natural habitats were eliminated. Midtown became a crisscross of streets dotted with vernacular bungalows and cottages. Oceanfront settings were readied as stages for more impressive houses. When hotel guests returned at the beginning of the 1913 season, they found fewer trails and footpaths. Instead, they beheld three subdivisions with streets planned for as many as two-hundred houses, two banks, three newspapers, commercial lots selling at $200 a front foot, a new toll bridge, and a scenic ocean road.

Above. The Royal Park subdivision. *Historical Society of Palm Beach County.*

Below. Royal Palm Way served as the main thoroughfare of the Royal Park subdivision, extending from the ocean to a lakeside bridge that linked pedestrian and automobile traffic with West Palm Beach. *Historical Society of Palm Beach County.*

LINED UP AT GATE OF GULF STREAM BOULEVARD

Photo by Turnage

SCENE IMMEDIATELY PRIOR TO THE OPENING OF THE GATE OF THIS MAGNIFICENT DRIVEWAY
ALONG THE ATLANTIC'S COAST ON SATURDAY, JANUARY 22, 1916

Above. Big cars, big houses, big jewels, big hedges, and big prices reflected the "bigger-the-better" maxim that was Palm Beach's calling card. *Historical Society of Palm Beach County.*

Below. Soon after the 1916 opening of the ocean boulevard from Palm Beach to Delray Beach, Palm Beach residents complained the scenic roadway attracted too many rubberneckers. *Palm Beach Post photo file.*

"The automobile will figure in Palm Beach life this season for the first time," predicted *The New York Times* in January 1913. The resort would now be "... accessible to those other than have great wealth," The Times declared.

Nearly sixty days after he left Boston by car, Clarke Boynton drove across the Royal Park Bridge on January 10, 1913. Having experienced numerous blowouts while being pulled by mules from mud holes in nearly every southern state, the intrepid trailblazer crossed rivers aboard ferries and rafts. Once on Palm Beach, he was able to park his automobile in a garage at the foot of the railroad bridge on Main Street across from Bradley's Beach Club. Originally built in 1906 to house wheel chairs and a few horseless carriages, the Flagler-owned facility had begun making room for as many as one-hundred automobiles.

Four years after work began, the last leg of the epic ocean road was finally completed from Palm Beach to Delray. A three-mile parade of one-hundred fifty cars inaugurated "the state's finest highway," viewed along the route by more than one thousand spectators. Making for the greatest gathering of automobiles in Palm Beach County's history, the motorcade assembled at Royal Palm Way and proceeded south. At the Bingham's Figulus estate, the road abruptly curved west toward the lake before bending back along the ocean at the Croker estate, later known as Widener's Curve. Having triggered awareness for motoring as a recreation, hundreds of visitors ordered their cars brought down to the Royal Poinciana Hotel and The Breakers. Florida was proclaimed a mecca for automobilists. Within a short time, taking a ride south to Delray became a bumper-to-bumper distraction. Soon, Palm Beach residents would complain the ocean road was a nuisance, filled with rubberneckers.

Pittsburgh steel magnate Henry Phipps was one of the first buyers along Palm Beach's new beach road, spurring a boom for oceanfront parcels where previously the lakeside was the preferred location. A *New York Times* headline proclaimed, "New Yorker will build three villas there for his family." For a reported purchase price of $90,000, Phipps acquired one-thousand feet of ocean-to-lake property in the town's North End. On property south of what was then the Florida Gun Club that a few years later would become the Palm Beach Country Club, Phipps announced plans for three houses to be built for his children, Henry Carnegie Phipps, Amy Phipps Guest and John S. Phipps.

The big wave

The building craze that took hold on Palm Beach before the Great War was resumed with a fervor after the Armistice was signed in 1918. An even more enormous economic boom resulted in further mansion building. For more than a decade, the value of Palm Beach's annual building permits rivaled those of the state's largest cities.

By 1921 once dusty sand trails and shell-rocked paths were now made of brick, asphalt and concrete. Road building struggled to keep up with the state's now seventy-four-thousand motor cars. On Palm Beach, the Everglades Club added a parking garage to its amenities. Worth Avenue featured Rolls Royce, Cadillac and Packard showrooms next to fashionable dress salons and jewelers. With Golf View Road reported to have more Rolls Royce owners than anywhere else in the world, the English auto manufacturer added a garage with a full-time mechanic on Royal Palm Way.

"Jungle Trail is to be destroyed, succumbing to home hunters," decried a February 1923 headline, indicating the continued loss of what two decades earlier was Palm Beach's main attraction. With the platting and development of El Bravo Park south of the Everglades Club golf course, the town's oldest and largest remaining collection of gumbo limbo, live oaks, mangroves, and cabbage palms was destroyed.

After a decade of developers supplanting habitats with Spanish patios and Italian courtyards, Palm Beach's unceasing growth was thwarted by a combination of events resulting in a more disconnected pattern of development. As much as the 1930s economic U-turn and 1940s war restrictions influenced the resort's architectural style and scale, a series of storms during the late 1920s caused drastic changes to the Palm Beach landscape.

The Hurricane of 1926 took thirty to forty feet of coastline, causing severe damage to the South End. The more destructive Hurricane of 1928 eroded seventy to eighty feet, bringing about a complete collapse of Ocean Boulevard from Palm Beach to Delray Beach that would take years to rebuild. The shore road's subsequent reconfiguration became one the town's most bitterly contested issues.

Above. Hotel Alba, North Lake Trail. December, 1925. *Historical Society of Palm Beach County.*

Below. During the 1930s the Alba-Ambassador Hotel was renamed the Palm Beach Biltmore. In 1981, it was converted into a 128-unit condominium. *Augustus Mayhew Photography.*

Above. After the 1928 hurricane, North Ocean Boulevard residents from El Mirasol to the Palm Beach Country Club were able to permanently close the roadway. *Library of Congress.*

Below. With the completion of the new Flagler Bridge in 1938, the town's Main Street was widened and renamed Royal Poinciana Way. *Historical Society of Palm Beach County.*

North vs. South

In the years following the Hurricane of 1928, oceanfront property owners in the North End from Wells Road to the inlet were successful in having the heavily damaged ocean road permanently closed in front of their homes. The influential group, headed by E. T. Stotesbury, president of the Palm Beach Taxpayer's Alliance, counted Charles Munn, Gurnee Munn, John S. Phipps, and Henry Phipps, among their membership. They argued the repair of the ocean road was a tax burden. After a contentious debate lasting several years, the group's offer to pay for the widening and beautification of Palm Beach Avenue, also known as the County Road, was accepted. By the early 1930s, these residents had converted North County Road service entrances into their estates' primary ingress.

Also, after the 1928 storm, the Garden Club of Palm Beach introduced its Town Plan that led to the creation of a Planning and Zoning Board. While several key parts of the plan were instituted, some components were abandoned and never implemented. The plan for keeping an oceanfront pathway open between Wells Road and the Palm Beach Country Club for pedestrians and wheelchairs was never realized. For the Stotesbury's at El Mirasol, Treanor and Fatio designed an imposing new entrance portal during the early 1930s, adding a notable architectural presence along the town's re-engineered County Road gateway to the North End.

South End property owners, however, from Vita Serena to what is now known as Gulfstream Drive, were not offered the same arrangement that transformed their North End counterparts' estates into oceanfront enclaves. Led by Harold S. Vanderbilt, these property owners were at first assured they would receive similar treatment. Although a bond issue was passed to rebuild the ocean road in front of their homes, property owners were reportedly misled, believing the town would intervene and insist traffic be rerouted along the County Road.

Vanderbilt declared his gentleman's agreement with Mayor Barclay Warburton should supersede the interests of the county and state road departments. The resulting rancor and political backpedaling caused Vanderbilt to sell El Solano, his Mizner-designed mansion on South Ocean Boulevard, and move to Manalapan where later he became mayor.

The 1928 storm also washed out the three-mile stretch of road south of

Sloan's Curve. It was repaired and kept in its original scenic location. After being patched-up, the road was lost again to a smaller storm and closed for two years. Repaved again, it would be considered a complete loss following the 1947 storm. At that time, the entire stretch of Ocean Boulevard from Sloan's Curve to Manalapan's Chillingworth's Curve was permanently shut down and rerouted along the lakefront. During the succeeding decade, the road's relocation made room for rows of apartment buildings and their successors, multi-story condominiums.

Twists and turns

Just as Ocean Boulevard was restyled into something unrecognizable from its picturesque origins, the town's Main Street was supersized into a thoroughfare. With the dismantling of the railroad tracks and the demolition of the train station, the new four-lane Flagler Memorial Bridge motorway opened in July 1938. A royal palm lined parkway named Royal Poinciana Way featured two fifty-foot lanes divided by a sixty-nine-foot center park dotted with yellow buttercups and bordered by seven-and-one-half-foot-wide sidewalks.

The ad hoc development of North Lake Way and the Lake Trail grew with as many twists and turns as curves along Ocean Boulevard. The roadway's path was frequently rerouted as much by seasonal flooding as by developers who gained approvals for housing sites by filling in low-lying marshes and swamps. In 1923 residents were warned that fire trucks would be allowed on the pedestrian path as there was no other access to several lakefront properties. The pedestrian walkway and the motorway were also subject to decades of conflicts over right-of-ways. Some lakefront residents blockaded the pedestrian trail, leading them into lengthy court fights with the town. It wasn't until the early 1940s when agreements were reached with the Palm Beach Country Club and Anna Dodge Dillman, owner of Playa Riente, permitting a continuation of Lake Way to the far North End.

Design detour

In his article "Revolt at Palm Beach," published in a Fall 1935 issue of House Beautiful magazine, local historian Louis Capron declared there had been a seismic shift in architectural style away from the previous decade's appreciation for Spanish and Italian motifs. Capron wrote that during the winter of 1933-1934, island architects began adapting the Tropical Colonial

A Masterpiece of Design and Construction
. . . PLANNED, BUILT AND BEAUTIFIED BY AMERICA'S GREAT NAMES

JOHN HANS GRAHAM, Architect, A.I.A., known throughout Europe and America for his brilliant hotel designing, has created in the Towers a perfect blend of building and site to serve modern, functional living.

TAYLOR CONSTRUCTION CO., Miami, Florida, Builders, are the nation's largest hotel builders. Prior to erecting the Towers, their recent assignments included construction of the fabulous Eden Roc and Fountainbleau Hotels, and the new Americana in Miami Beach.

In providing for the interior beauty and convenience of the Towers, only the finest appointments in quality and taste have been chosen. MARTHA BARNES, Interior Designer, N. Y., has created stunning effects throughout, using BORIS KROLL fabrics and coordinating colors in the lobby and restaurant with the specially designed, hand-loomed carpet by EUGENE FIELDS CO. The handsome chandeliers were designed by HARRY GITLIN and executed by STAMFORD LIGHTING CO. Specially designed furniture for various suites is from JOHN STUART, INC. All refrigerators, built-in ovens and surface cookers are color-coordinated units by ADMIRAL CORP. All carpets throughout the corridors and suites are by BIGELOW-SANFORD CARPET CO. Furnishings have been executed and installed by R. MARS, THE CONTRACT CO., Washington, D. C.

NEW YORK TIMES, 1956

Above. Palm Beach Towers. *New York Times*, advertisement. 1956. *Palm Beach Towers Collection.*

Above. The President of Palm Beach offered apartment owners full hotel services until 1970 when it was converted into a condominium. *Augustus Mayhew Photography*.

style first introduced the previous decade by Howard Major on Peruvian Avenue at Major Alley, the architect's attached cluster of mixed residential types.

Capron pointed out Bermuda influences could be found in the emerging Georgian, Southern Colonial, Monterey, and British West Indies style houses, specifically Major's West Indian Neoclassical design for George Jessel and the eighteenth century French-inspired mansion for Bernard Kroger by Volk and Maas. These less theatrical treatments, designed more to be lived in than to impress passers-by or party-goers, shared structural similarities in their use of balconies, verandahs, window types, and shutters.

In 1937, when Town Hall issued permits for sixty-six houses totaling more than $2.4 million, the most popular locations for new construction were the North End's Inlet subdivision, Pendleton Avenue, Cocoanut Grove, and North Lake Trail. The year's most expensive permit for $165,000 was issued to E. F. Hutton for the construction of Four Winds, then known as the town's largest frame house.

Even as the threat of World War II grew, new construction continued. During the fall of 1940, Mary Benjamin Rogers was having an investment house built on Chilean Avenue's lake block, designed by architect Belford Shoumate. The following year, forty houses were built, though not large country club houses.

Where building never ends

In May 1945, E. R. Bradley, proprietor of the sky's-the-limit casino at the Beach Club, announced his landmark destination would be torn down for a park. Following the end of World War II, gambling on Palm Beach took on a different meaning with the escalation of the resort's flourishing building and real estate industry. The lifting of wartime restrictions and an increasing supply of materials turned 1947 and 1948 into banner years for construction. On Sunrise Avenue east of the Paramount Theatre, the sixty-room Carlton Hotel was built for $500,000. The lakefront Beaux Arts shopping center, designed by August Geiger in 1917, was converted into a twenty-four unit apartment house. The Colony movie theater opened on Sunrise Avenue west of County Road. Even the pier, newly renamed the Palm Beach Pier, was enhanced with a cocktail lounge, widened promenade deck and a smart restaurant.

The Phipps family's commercial development interests, Bessemer Properties and the Palm Beach Company, continued to subdivide and develop its extensive holdings. In Midtown, Bessemer resumed development of Everglades Island, interrupted by the war. In the North End near the inlet, Phipps interests subdivided estates with residential building lots. South of Widener's Curve, a Phipps-related company acquired the vast oceanfront parcel that once made up the Croker estate and various ocean-to-lake parcels as far south as the Lake Worth Bridge.

In 1950, Bessemer acquired the Royal Poinciana Hotel property from the Florida East Coast Hotel company for a commercial development. The following year, the company sold a small parcel along Cocoanut Row for a bank site and installed a twelve-hundred-eighty-two-foot seawall extending from Whitehall to the Flagler Memorial Bridge. Shortly thereafter, Bessemer sold the former landmark hotel property to the developers of the $5.5 million Palm Beach Towers hotel-apartment complex, acknowledged as the largest hotel-apartment complex in Florida. To the south of Sloan's Curve, where the ocean road was rerouted along the lakefront, Bessemer's development potential doubled, making for sites on both sides of the new road. Across from what became Phipps Park, Bessemer filled in an island and platted Ibis Isle in 1953.

The post-World War II era also introduced another stylistic about face. Unlike the 1930s, when modernist houses stood alongside the borrowed motifs from the Spanish and Italian Renaissance, several of the island's great mansions were demolished, supplanted by rows of subdivision houses with modern conveniences. In 1955, sixty-four new residential building permits were issued. Samuel Peck's new $208,000 home on Jungle Road was the year's largest permit.

"Anyone who doesn't think Palm Beach is growing should examine our records," said Edward Ehringer Jr., the town's chief building inspector. "From 1945 to 1955, the annual totals for building permits have increased from $1 million to $6 million," Ehringer added. By 1956, building permits were issued for more than ten million dollars. Palm Beach was again posting construction records.

Six years later, building permits outrivaled those in 1925, considered the resort's greatest construction period when The Breakers and The Alba-

Above. Built in the late 1960s as "the town's most expensive rental apartments," the 242-unit Sun & Surf complex replaced the private Sun & Surf Beach Club. *Augustus Mayhew Photography.*

Below. The Breakers cottages were demolished to make room for multi-story apartment buildings. *Historical Society of Palm Beach County.*

Above. Built in 1978, the Dunster House condominium is one of several Midtown condominiums overlooking the town's public beach. *Augustus Mayhew Photography.*

Biltmore were built. In 1962, $20 million in concrete, steel and wood was poured onto the island, highlighted by the ninety-six-unit The President in the South End, the six-story Florida Capital Building at Royal Palm Way, the sixty-four-unit 400 Building in Midtown, and the sixty-unit Lake Towers apartments, built for $1.6 million on North Lake Way. Under the headline "Luxury Building Boom," the *Palm Beach Daily News* reported at year's end, "Palm Beach has never grown so fast and so high as in 1962."

It wasn't until 1969 that residents grew weary of the town's building upsurge. "Building Boom Perturbs Palm Beach Civic Group," read a local headline, as the need for a building moratorium gained support. Despite new limitations, the Town Council granted exceptions and allowed building permits to reach record highs. By the beginning of the next decade, more than twenty-five-thousand cars daily crossed the Flagler Memorial Bridge between Palm Beach and West Palm Beach. A 1973 zoning change converted Royal Palm Way from predominately residential to commercial, paving the way for multi-story office buildings. "What was at one time one of the most beautiful streets in Palm Beach has been quartered and skewered," wrote resident Whitney Cushing, who described the zoning change as "the last nail in the coffin."

Hard hats, Black ties and Ball gowns

Just as Gilded Age mansion builders and real estate speculators ushered in the twentieth century, the echo of Flagler's "Pay-no-matter-the-price!" remains Palm Beach's mantra for its ongoing twenty-first century real estate boom. Some houses have been bought and sold so often that neighbors claim garages stow moving vans and house entrances are equipped with revolving doors. Ironically, the same development interests that once claimed smaller, more modern houses were most suitable for Palm Beach, would several decades later demolish those houses and replace them with larger variations of the houses they once destroyed.

Whatever the forgotten aspects that may have first brought the fortunate few to Palm Beach's now vanished jungle, the tireless yen for the bigger-the-better has displaced the sentiment for the familiarity and acceptance of the status quo. For as long as the business of Palm Beach is building, and residents opt to remember the past rather than live with it, the island's appeal remains its ever-changing, unsettled landscape.

Above & Below. In March 1911 pioneer aviator John A. D. McCurdy made history when he flew a Curtiss biplane over Palm Beach transmitting the world's first radio messages between an aircraft and a ground station. According to reports, McCurdy was then arrested for flying on Sunday, "in violation of The Lord's Day." *State of Florida Archive.*

2

HIGH OVER PALM BEACH

Air ships, boat planes and aerial yachts were buzzing above Ocean Boulevard and the Lake Trail more than a century before present-day private and commercial jets became a routine part of Palm Beach's sound levels. At the forefront of the nation's pre-World War I commercial and military aviation development, the flying machines sailing over Lake Worth became as much a part of the seasonal allure as wheelchair rides, cakewalks and fashion parades.

On Saturday, February 25, 1911, at 4:16 p.m., John Arthur Douglas McCurdy piloted the area's first powered aircraft flight, making a circular flight around Lake Worth that soared one-thousand feet above the Royal Poinciana Hotel. During this pioneering flight, the world's first wireless message was sent from a plane to the ground. The four-minute hop took off and landed from the newly opened Bethesda Park subdivision in West Palm Beach that had sponsored the aviation spectacle to spur real estate sales. Every afternoon for the next several weeks, the Curtiss Airplane Company's aerial exhibitions attracted the wheelchair brigade from Palm Beach, as well as bicycles and horseless carriages that gathered to marvel at the dips and glides.

Aviation takes off

Several years before the landmark Palm Beach flight, the Aerial Experiment Association (AEA) partnership was formed by Glenn Curtiss, Alexander Graham Bell and Bell's protégé, engineer John A. D. McCurdy, who was known as the ninth man in the world to fly an "air machine." In direct competition with the Wright Brothers ongoing aeronautical research, the AEA was founded to design and build commercially feasible aircraft with Curtiss as director of experiments, McCurdy as engineer and test pilot, and Bell as inventor extraordinaire. The group convened at Curtiss' motorcycle factory in Hammondsport, New York, where they first developed kite-like machines, naming them Red Wing, White Wing and June Bug, before designing more familiar aeronautic models.

When Curtiss organized the Curtiss Airplane Company in 1909, the Wrights sued for patent infringement, winning a judgment in their favor five years later. While the Wrights contributed to the technical essentials of aviation, they lacked the AEA's promotional skills in advancing aviation as a major industrial enterprise. Glenn Curtiss was the nation's first licensed pilot and trained the first woman pilot. He organized the first school of aviation, with several of the Wright brothers' original pilots, and started the first aeronautic exhibition company. Eventually, the Wright Aeronautical Corporation merged with the Curtiss Aeroplane and Engine Company. The Wright Brothers had been financed by Cornelius Vanderbilt III and August Belmont Jr. Glenn Curtiss's efforts were backed by Rodman Wanamaker.

Department store scion Rodman Wanamaker is credited with importing the first airplane to the United States, paying $2,200 in 1909 for a French Blériot. The family's New York department store became a showcase for some of aviation's notable milestones, from staging an early hot-air balloon lift-off from the Manhattan store's roof to being the first store with an airplane department, offering metal monoplanes for $25,000. A member of New York's Aero Club, Wanamaker established the annual Rodman Wanamaker Trophy, awarded to women who reached the highest altitude. Wanamaker's blank check was key to the Curtiss Company's success.

Within months of being launched, the AEA group achieved the first officially-recorded public flight. The development of the first seaplane soon followed. By 1909, the Curtiss motorcycle shop in Hammondsport was transformed into an airplane manufacturing plant for the Curtiss Aeroplane Company that then held ninety patents.

- Having introduced the first experimental seaplane flights in San Diego during the winter of 1910, the Curtiss Company came to Florida the

THE AMERICA
TRANS OCEANIC CO.

Agents for

HANGARS:	CURTISS	NEW YORK OFFICE:
Port Washington,		280 Madison Ave.,
Long Island	FLYING BOATS	New York City
Phone:	AEROPLANES	Phone:
Port Washington 364	AND MOTORS	Murray Hill 4997

Announces the opening of winter quarters on
Lake Worth, Palm Beach, Florida

Flying School   Demonstrations   Passenger Carrying

Above. A longtime supporter of aviation, Rodman Wanamaker was president of the America Trans-Oceanic Company that operated passenger seaplanes between Palm Beach and Long Island. *Library of Congress.*

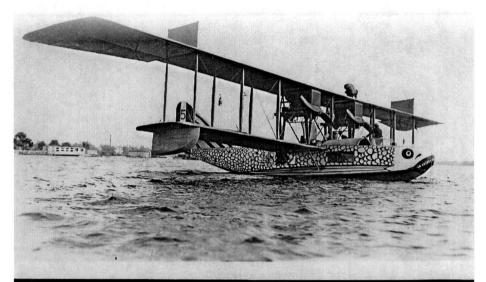

Above. The Big Fish flying boat carried twelve-passengers between Palm Beach, Miami and the Bahama Islands. *Historical Society of Palm Beach County.*

Below. A former United States Marine Corps aviator, Clifford L. Webster, left, was a pilot for the American Trans-Oceanic Company and the Curtiss Metropolitan Company operating flights from Long Island to Palm Beach. In April 1922, Webster's flight of a Loening air yacht between Palm Beach and New York broke the speed record. *Historical Society of Palm Beach County.*

following year. Newspaper ads offered a seaplane for $5,000 along with six- to eight-week pilot training classes for $600. After sponsored air shows in Daytona Beach and Miami's Biscayne Bay, they set off for Key West where they hoped to garner *The Havana Post* newspaper's $5,000 prize for the first successful two-hour ninety-six-mile Key West to Havana trip.

"McCurdy fails in flight over the seas from Key West to Havana; falls unhurt into the water," read front page headlines, when the plane crashed ten minutes from Havana harbor. Undaunted, Curtiss and his team of high fliers continued on to Palm Beach where their air shows captivated crowds along the lakefront, becoming the highlight of the 1911 social season. Because of Palm Beach's temperate winter climate and Lake Worth's accommodating natural setting, Palm Beach played a significant role as a seasonal proving ground for testing commercial and military aircraft, establishing several seaplane bases along the waterfront.

During the 1912 season, the Curtiss Aviation School was established in Miami, led by the school's director C. C. Witmer. In mid-January, aviator Barney Moran flew the first test of a seaplane over Biscayne Bay. Several days later, a Congressional delegation watched from the porch of the Royal Palm Hotel as Witmer made a flight around the bay. The Cuban government sent a student to enroll in the school's training classes. The same month, noted aviator Walter Brookins was thrilling Palm Beachers with his eight-cylinder bird machine.

The *Palm Beach Daily News* proclaimed the "Palm Beach Birds" were "the new king of outdoor sports." At the time, there were only ninety licensed pilots in the United States and as many as one-thousand passengers experienced air travel. Hundreds of spectators looked on as Walter Brookins took off from the railroad bridge, accompanied by the Royal Poinciana Hotel orchestra, and flew south to the Wigwam, Richard and Bula Crokers' estate in the South End, before circling back to land near the hotel docks. While some would only don scarves and goggles and pay to be photographed in front of the planes, others couldn't wait to take moonlight flights, albeit wearing bathing suits under their clothes in case of an unexpected dip into the ocean. Flying around Palm Beach became as popular a pastime as visiting the ostrich farm, with women among the most daring passengers.

Mrs. Arthur Wright professed "... when she was far beyond the water and land, she felt re-born and there was no sport that can prove its equal."

Mrs. George Jonas, the wife of Palm Beach's mayor, became so enthralled she wanted to study aeronautics immediately, so she could fly "whenever the fancy dictates." Mrs. John Shepherd, whose New Year's Day reception for several hundred was a Palm Beach institution, became the third woman to take flight at the resort.

By early February 1912, Curtiss opened a branch of his aviation school at Palm Beach. Robert Collins, president of the Aero Club of America, arrived to look over aviation's new focal point. "Lake Worth is just right for seaplanes," declared Collins. Along with the Burgess Company, Curtiss introduced three new types of seaplanes. Air shows were staged during the annual motor boat races on Lake Worth, as seaplanes utilized the dock in front of the Royal Poinciana Hotel.

Yet another significant impact occurred the following season when the US Army set up the Regional Corps Aviation School at the City Park in West Palm Beach, directly across from the Royal Poinciana Hotel. Six privates and twenty officers arrived for two months of pilot instructions. The government shipped the latest model seaplanes for training, constructing a hangar on the west side of the lake across from Royal Park and south of the Royal Palm Bridge.

At the Curtiss base, Frank Coffyn, one of the original seven Wright pilots, replaced Walter Brookins. In between "taking up society folks," Coffyn spent the season testing a sixty-horsepower, six-cylinder seaplane with a Sturtevant engine and a front hood shaped like the bow of a ship. Aviator William Thaw set a record at Palm Beach flying one mile in forty seconds. While he charged twenty dollars to take socialites as high as they wanted to go, his seaplane was said to have cost $65,000. By the time the school closed for the season and the planes were packed for their summer destinations, aviation on Palm Beach had become as thrilling a diversion as the high stakes gambling at Bradley's Beach Club casino.

The same year *Palm Beach Life* magazine added Aviation to its sport pages, detailing the who's who of the various comings-and-goings, Wanamaker and Curtiss formed the America Trans-Oceanic Company with plans for manufacturing the first plane to make a non-stop trans-Atlantic crossing. Though mechanical glitches and the onset of World War I thwarted the twin-engine *America's* flight, the partnership began a commercial airline passenger venture between Long Island and Palm Beach.

Lake Worth is
just right for seaplanes.

-Robert Collins, president of the Aero Club of America

Above. Grace Morrison, middle-row center, was the first president of the Women's Aeronautical Association that later became the foundation for the Palm Beach County Airport Association. Following Morrison's accidental death in 1936, the county's first major airport was named Morrison Field in her honor. *Historical Society of Palm Beach County*.

Above. As flying grew in popularity, the Curtiss Seaplane Base became one of the Palm Beach winter colony's favorite destinations. *Historical Society of Palm Beach County.*

The America Trans-Oceanic Company popularized flying from New York-to-Palm Beach. Passengers took off from a flying boat station at Peacock Point in Port Washington, New York, and landed ten hours later on Palm Beach's lakefront. The Rodman Wanamaker Flying School was set up in Port Washington. The company's hangar housed seven planes on the west side of Lake Worth north of the railroad bridge.

From its Palm Beach and Miami bases, Trans-Oceanic's flying boats flew to Nassau and Bimini in the Bahamas, and to Cuba. The company made four trips a week to Bimini. Six-passenger planes were used for joy hops to Miami. The Big Fish, a converted twelve-passenger Curtiss H-16 seaplane, was used for trips to the Bahamas and Havana. A moonlight flight left Palm Beach at five p.m. and arrived in Jacksonville five hours later. In November 1916, Curtiss decided to move his main aviation school in Newport News, Virginia, to Miami because of its stretch of beaches. In 1917, Atlantic City-Palm Beach was an eighteen-hour flight; by 1921, New York-Palm Beach took nine hours and fifty-six minutes with one fuel stop.

In January 1920, Rodman Wanamaker and five companions, including son-in-law Gurnee Munn, were adrift for twenty-six hours when his personal seaplane went down in the Atlantic between Palm Beach and Nassau. Upon their rescue, a *New York Times* story declared, "... flying to the Bahamas for a handshake with John Barleycorn was fast becoming the leading outdoor sport in these parts." As the 1920s Boom transformed Palm Beach, seaplane bases became a part of the Palm Beach landscape despite the aesthetic displeasure of The Garden Club of Palm Beach. Although the civic-minded group's 1929 Plan of Palm Beach recognized Lake Worth was an ideal airport for seaplanes and amphibians, they decreed service space, shelters and hangars must be hidden under the new proposed bridge.

By 1930 the sky above Palm Beach was said "to hum with a drone never before experienced," prompting the Town Council to adopt an ordinance prohibiting seaplanes from taking-off or landing in the Lake Worth yacht harbor between the Flagler Bridge and the Royal Park Bridge. Violations would result in a $500 fine and not more than sixty days in jail. At the same time, work on Roosevelt Field neared completion in West Palm Beach. The Curtiss-Wright Company and the Roosevelt Flying Service agreed to expand the seaplane base on the east shore of Lake Worth north of the railroad bridge. Additionally, a one-hundred-fifty-foot by one-hundred-fifty-foot ramp, new hangar and shop were built adjacent to the existing base the Curtiss Company had operated during the previous two years on the west side of the lake. As a result, the enlarged and renovated seaplane bases would complement the two new landing fields with border lights and night beacons, patterned after Roosevelt Field on Long Island. The expanded venture would be staffed with an operations manager, a traffic manager, eight mechanics, and five pilots.

Shortly before his death during the summer of 1930, Glenn Curtiss moved his aviation schools to his Hialeah-based Florida Aviation Camp and deeded a one-hundred-sixty-acre tract to the City of Miami, previously leased to the city as a temporary air field in the northern part of Hialeah. By 1951, the airport stretched over three thousand acres and accommodated fifty-nine airlines. Today, it is known as the Miami International Airport.

In 1937, the Palm Beach Seaplane Base at Bethesda Park was one of three airplane ports in Florida and one of twelve in the United States. On Palm Beach, the seaplane base at Royal Park was converted into the town's South Lake Drive development adjacent to the Brazilian Avenue docks. While residents, including Michael Phipps and Grover Whalen, kept private seaplanes docked at their North Lake Way properties for many years, in 1982 the Town of Palm Beach made it unlawful for any aircraft to take-off or land in the water of Lake Worth within the town's corporate limits, closing a chapter on one of Palm Beach's most unique pleasures.

Above. The Glenn H. Curtiss Aviation Museum in Hammondsport, New York, houses many of the "aerial yachts" and seaplanes that turned Palm Beach's lakefront into a runway where take-offs and landings were commonplace. *Augustus Mayhew Photography.*

Above. Ernest H. Histed's photograph of Henry M. Flagler was taken in 1909. Having studied photography with a protégé of Daguerre's, Histed equipped his studios with the latest electric lights, promising "clients made bright even on dull foggy days." *Historical Society of Palm Beach County.*

3

ABOUT FACE
PORTRAITS FROM PARADISE

By the time the Royal Poinciana Hotel held its first Washington's Birthday Ball, portrait painters and photographers had already opened studios at Palm Beach, adding the American Riviera to their other ateliers in ritzy cosmopolitan quarters and summer resorts. Who better to flatter Belle Époque's grandeur — besides jewelers and couturiers — than society painters and photographers trained to smooth the fine line between illusion and reality, so often blurred in Palm Beach?

Over the ensuing decades, they and their predecessors painted and snapped away — and for good reason. "People have more time to pose in resorts," confided artist Richard Banks, before his one-man show featuring Social Register notables opened in 1966 at Lillian Phipps Galleries on Palm Beach, a place suspended in a perpetual spring where time is measured by episodic seasons. Banks' observation about the idle rich was as prevalent a perception then as it was following the Civil War when top-hat tycoons turned conspicuous consumption into a profession. Daguerreotypes were stashed in the attic, replaced with impressive Gilded Age portraits by John Singer Sargent and Philip de László. These essential status symbols hung above every millionaire's Fifth Avenue drawing room fireplace.

While philanthropy fulfills much of today's pursuit for immortality, yesterday's fat cats and bigwigs indulged in portrait sittings. Although portraiture might appear as productive as twiddling thumbs or sun bathing, its outcome, at the least, created a conversation piece; at the most, an artful legacy. Collectively, Palm Beach's portrait artists were among the twentieth century's most impressive aestheticians, known for enhancing the character and characteristics of their subjects.

Focus on Palm Beach

The renowned English-born photographer Ernest Walter Histed was among the first to set up a tripod on the Jungle Trail near the Royal Poinciana Hotel, bringing with him a client list topped by England's nobility and Europe's royal crowns. Much like the great painters, he was known simply as "Histed." Upon his arrival in New York and Newport where Vanderbilts, du Ponts, and Wideners were his subjects, Histed was proclaimed the most artistic portraitist in America. His "subtleties of light and shadow lay bare for inspection the real man or woman behind the human mask," according to *Metropolitan* magazine.

Above Left. J. Clinton Shepherd, self-portrait. *J. Clinton Shepherd family.*

Above Right. Channing Hare executed this sketch of Consuelo Vanderbilt Balsan, the former Duchess of Marlborough. Beginning in the 1940s, Hare reigned as the town's most popular portraitist for more than three decades. *Ellen Glendinning Ordway Collection.*

Having studied photography with a protégé of Daguerre's, Histed accommodated patrons for either at-home sittings or at studios on Fifth Avenue in New York, the Casino in Newport, or Forty-two Baker Street, London, equipped with the latest electric lights promising "clients made bright even on dull foggy days." A September 1909 *Town & Country* magazine article reported "... that Histed is a genius has long been conceded. He is now seldom referred to as a photographer but as a portraitist."

Eventually on Palm Beach, Histed moved to a studio near Phipps Plaza before gaining more exposure with a location on Worth Avenue. His secret was said to be his Platinotype finish, capable of transforming the look of an unimpressive provincial czar into an imposing international titan. By using platinum in his prints, Histed's portraits were guaranteed to never fade and always look as if they were made yesterday.

Sometime after Histed's arrival, William Louis Koehne, a prominent society photographer in Chicago and Newport since the 1890s, made the unspoiled tropical island his winter destination. A familiar Palm Beach character for more than fifty years, Koehne and his wife Zila spent their first several seasons at the Royal Poinciana Hotel and The Breakers before acquiring an oceanfront lot in 1911 on Peruvian Avenue. There they built Zila Villa, one of Palm Beach's most significant architectural landmarks, with a photographic studio and darkroom.

"The wonderful lighting effects obtainable in Palm Beach cannot be equaled anywhere in the world," declared Koehne in his newspaper ads. He invited prospective clients to visit his unique Prairie Modern style seaside studio that became known as The Fishbowl because of its large glass windows and doors. The Koehnes enjoyed non-stop teas and dinners, making headlines when they staged a wedding for monkeys, photographed in costumes apropos for a marriage ceremony and reception.

Painting the town

During the spring of 1917, Paris Singer bought a house on Peruvian Avenue across from the Koehne's villa and studio. Several years later, it was Singer who introduced to Palm Beach one of England's best known portrait painters, Sir Oswald Birley. "Nowhere in the world have I seen so luminous quality of light as there is in Palm Beach," declared Sir Oswald, who was ensconced in a multi-story studio-villa built for him on the grounds of the

Everglades Club overlooking Singer Basin and Lake Worth. Though Birley remains best known for his portraits of Paris Singer and E. T. Stotesbury, during the 1925 season an exhibition of his portrayals of English and American notables was staged in the Music Room at Whitehall. Sir Oswald's work prompted a favorable response resulting in a considerable number of new commissions. A presence in Palm Beach for more than twenty-five years, during the late 1950s he was a houseguest at Mar-a-Lago where he painted Joseph Davies.

Above. Channing Hare. *Ellen Glendinning Ordway Collection.*

At the same time Sir Oswald's easel was on the move on Palm Beach, New York and Chicago portraitist William van Dresser also made his Palm Beach debut in February 1925 at Whitehall. Initially sponsored by Eva Stotesbury, van Dresser maintained studios on Via Parigi and Phipps Plaza. In addition to Harold Vanderbilt, Howard Phipps, Billie Burke, Grover Whalen, Addison Mizner, and a host Palm Beach families, the artist did portraits of President Calvin Coolidge and President Franklin D. Roosevelt. In 1929, van Dresser conceived and appeared in a short film shown at the Beaux-Arts Theater titled "Shady Lady" where he demonstrated and explained the process of making a portrait.

Celebrated for his charcoal sketches, pastel renderings and sanguine drawings, van Dresser produced hundreds of portraits during his twenty years on Palm Beach before moving in 1940 to Wild Cat Bend, his home-studio in Boca Raton. During the war years at a studio located at the Boca Raton Club, he held life drawing classes for wives of army men.

La Folie de Monvel

"My father bartered his commission for a portrait of me," said Alex Fatio Taylor, whose father Maurice Fatio, principal of the Treanor & Fatio architectural firm in Palm Beach, designed French portrait artist Bernard Boutet de Monvel's unique octagonal house-studio on Hi-Mount Road in 1937.

Son of painter Maurice Boutet de Monvel, the precocious artist's illustrations appeared in several periodicals before developing an exclusive presence at Harper's Bazaar from 1926 to 1933. He came to Palm Beach as a houseguest at Thatchcote, the home of Mrs. Mary Benjamin Rogers, an accomplished artist and the first wife of Standard Oil heir Henry H. Rogers Jr. Within a month, de Monvel began planning his own house, said to be his fifth.

For de Monvel, the Swiss-educated architect designed a unique octagonal house with north light situated on a private bluff atop the town's highest elevations. The architect combined a centrally located octagonal living room-studio flanked by four square rooms with terraces on three sides providing views of the lake, the golf course and the ocean.

During the 1937 season, The Society of the Four Arts held a major exhibition of de Monvel's portraits, pastels and murals. The showcase featured thirty-four paintings including portraits of Mrs. Vincent Astor, Fernanda Wanamaker Munn, Mary Benjamin Rogers and her daughter Millicent Rogers, Lady Mendl, Marquesa de Cuevas, Mona Williams, and Anita Young. In addition, there were five sketches for life-size portraits, highlighted by images of the Maharajah of Indore and Prince Sixte de Bourbon.

In October 1949 de Monvel was killed in an airplane crash on a flight from Paris to New York. La Folie de Monvel was sold to another accomplished artist Gertrude Schweitzer who worked and lived there for nearly forty years. While many of Boutet de Monvel's portraits are still in museum condition, only the Fatio-designed octagonal main room remains of the artist's Palm Beach folly. Despite being designated a local landmark in 1990, the one-of-a-kind house's secondary extensions were removed.

Portrait galleries

When Channing Hare came to Palm Beach during the early 1940s, he leased La Folie de Monvel where he entertained the town's A-list. Reigning as the town's most popular portraitist for three decades, Hare's first exhibition was at the venerable Worth Avenue Gallery, managed by Mary Benson and owned by Alice de Lamar. The gallery also represented portrait sculptor Stuart Benson and Zoe Shippen, well known for her children's portraits. Shippen was so popular on Palm Beach that she was reported to be the second person a new mother called after the obstetrician.

Local art writers described Hare's talent "to portray a person not a physique" and "to express the human mystery by revealing worlds of personality by unusual angles of vision, notably by painting figures where the face is turned away from the audience, the eyes not hidden, but rather withheld from view while the individuality is expressed in a gesture of the shoulder, a curve of the back, and an arabesque of the neck."

During the 1940s, the spotlight also focused on portraits by Kyril Vassilev, a Russian-born Old Master-styled painter whose renderings of Sam and Goldie Paley, Amy Guest and Mona Williams made his signature pieces popular. In 1943, Vassilev was evicted from his Worth Avenue studio when it was discovered he was raising homing pigeons. After he moved his studio to Sunset Avenue, he was once again dislodged when town officials cited him for breeding Doberman pinschers. Exiled to West Palm Beach, Vassilev and his wife Rosa Tusa, food editor at *The Palm Beach Post*, were well-liked members of local art circles.

Rather than representing themselves, the Worth Avenue Gallery, Palm Beach Gallery, Wally Findlay and James Hunt Barker represented many of the period's portrait artists. In 1965, Palm Beach Galleries staged an exhibition of portrait artists featuring Charles Baskerville, Simon Elwes, Trafford Klotts, Peggy Reventlow, and Alejo Vidal-Quadras.

Dominick Dunne called Alejo Vidal-Quadras the "Boldoni of Palm Beach." Having pleased royal families and jet set notables from Barcelona to Buenos Aires with his palette of charcoal, pastel and oil portraits, Vidal-Quadras, as much a craftsman as an artist, made his first appearance at Wally Findlay Gallery in 1964. Credited a decade later with more than two-thousand portraits, the artist's work, though intentionally devoid of backgrounds, became known for its "gracefulness, distinction, and sensitivity."

Through the looking glass

For all of their candid disclosures about their subjects and their work, no other portrait artist rivaled photographer, painter, author, and Academy Award-winning designer Cecil Beaton's candid observations about Palm Beach matrons found in the book, *The Unexpurgated Beaton: The Cecil Beaton Diaries as He Wrote Them, 1970 -1980*. With carte blanche into the worlds of stage, screen, and society, Beaton's reputation was set when in 1937 he was the official photographer for the wedding of Wallis Simpson and the Duke of Windsor, as well as the official photographer at Queen Elizabeth II's coronation in 1953.

During the 1970s, Beaton came to Palm Beach at the behest of the James Hunt Barker Gallery that set up commissioned portraits for him to paint and photograph. During his initial foray into the depths of Palm Beach society, he was a houseguest at Gemini, Loel and Gloria Guinness' oceanfront estate in Manalapan, where Beaton found cushions and plates inscribed with comic mottos. In the guest room, a plate was etched with the message: "When the hosts are drinking and they invite you to stay until Tuesday, remember they don't mean it."

While Beaton considered it "an excellent way of killing a day," Beaton's diary entries portray Palm Beach's dames and dowagers in search of a sympathetic mirror:

"I set up my roughly improvised painting materials and embark on a huge representation of the unknown lady in front of me. She was a tired and pathetic over middle-aged woman with a rich widow as a mother. While I drew, her mother prepared lunch for her pet poodle."

"Carola Mandel, a Cuban who never stopped talking about being the greatest shot in the world with five-hundred trophies. She wished to be portrayed in an evening dress with long kid gloves, a dozen silver trophies, and a gun. Six hours later, I had perpetrated a monstrous picture."

"She was togged up in the glad rags of a Twenties kewpie doll with a peppermint pink chiffon mini-evening dress, bobbed hair, and a scarlet mouth."

Four years later as a photographer, and a guest at Charles and Jayne Wrightsman's estate, Beaton wrote: "Mrs. Rose Kennedy was on the telephone, wanting to know if she should wear false eyelashes. She giggled when I told her not to get flustered … She is publicity mad and thrilled to appear for the first time in *Vogue*."

"Jayne Wrightsman appeared in a head scarf, obviously just had her face lifted. She was without lines, smooth, shiny, and siliconed up to her eyes. However, I don't think it's a bad job; probably an improvement," Beaton wrote. "Jayne has made the place beautiful with the best decorators and highest museum quality furniture. Altogether, there are fourteen servants indoors, at least six outside, and Jules, the giant French chauffeur," he added.

As today's portrait artists have lost cultural ground to wealth managers, personal trainers and real estate agents, Cecil Beaton's quip might characterize the ambiance when a becoming image of one's self was a fashionable conceit. "Palm Beach — it is a world apart, a hangover from when privilege was everything."

Above. Artist Bernard Boutet de Monvel painted Gladys "Gaggy" Quentell Reed's portrait in 1935. The French artist was popular portraitist of Palm Beach's society women, including Fernanda Wanamaker Munn, Lady Mendl, Anita Young, and Mona Williams. *Private collection*.

Above. Palm Beach was a setting for several motion pictures as illustrated by this of the cast and crew of The Palm Beach Girl starring Bebe Daniels filming near The Breakers beach and pier. *Historical Society of Palm Beach County.*

Below. Not only was Palm Beach the setting for making films and rubbing elbows with Hollywood moguls and screen idols but also at one time the town had four movie theaters, including the Garden Theatre on Main Street. *Historical Society of Palm Beach County.*

4

LIGHTS! CAMERA! ACTION!
SOCIETY FILMS ON
OCEAN BOULEVARD

During the 1916 and 1917 season, the First World War's ongoing conflict weighed heavily on Palm Beach's cottage colony, however much the sound of champagne corks popping along the beach boardwalk at The Breakers might have appeared indifferent to the rat-a-tat-tat of machine guns in the South of France.

With the United States threatened by German U-boats, and already unofficially at war with the Central Powers, society swells armed themselves with their most powerful weapon — their checkbook. Although proceeds from the Golf Ball and the Tennis Ball were earmarked to fund the building of a local hospital, Eva Stotesbury, Owen Kenan, and Tessie Oelrichs organized benefits to aid British and French allies, even before the United States formally entered combat.

The Charity Ball at the Royal Poinciana Hotel attracted several thousand patriotic supporters to assist the International Red Cross efforts. The Duchess of Richelieu's musical soiree at The Breakers contributed to the welfare of France's growing number of tubercular soldiers. One of Palm Beach's most recent habitués, Paris Singer, converted his one-hundred-room mansion on the English Riviera into a military hospital. Harold S. Vanderbilt resigned as rear commodore of the New York Yacht Club to enlist as a lieutenant in the US Naval Reserves, guarding Newport's coastline.

Nonetheless, bluebloods and millionaires unable or reluctant to don uniforms made national headlines when they were cast in what was called a society motion picture with a cameraman and five-thousand feet of film donated by William Randolph Hearst, a regular guest at The Breakers. By participating in "strictly a Palm Beach play" with all scenes filmed on Palm Beach, more than fifty members of Bradley's Beach Club would take time away from the roulette table to express their patriotism by raising much needed funds for the American Ambulance Field Service Corps in France.

Although footage from these vanity silent film productions appears to be lost, the newspaper accounts about *The Island of Happiness* and *The Isle of Tomorrow* provide a fascinating glimpse into society's penchant for make-believe and inclination to be "camera-wise." The productions were reported to have shown "… just how men and women in the innermost circle of fashionable society walk, dance, talk, munch sandwiches, balance a cup of tea, swing a cane, and the thousand-and-one-things which are a mystery to the average bystander."

The Island of Happiness

On a Saturday evening in early March 1916, one of the largest crowds ever assembled on Palm Beach gathered in the dining room at the Royal Poinciana Hotel to watch *The Island of Happiness*, a silent film directed by Pearl White, star of the serial classic *Perils of Pauline*.

Among the throng who paid a three-dollar admission charge were the film's star, Marie Louise Wanamaker Munn, and her supporting cast recruited from the Social Register. The previous year, Munn had made her screen debut when her marriage to Gurnee Munn was filmed at Lindenhurst, the Wanamaker family estate. The one-thousand feet of film provided the first private event "seen by the eye of a motion picture camera" in Philadelphia, according to *Motion Picture World* magazine.

The film's demanding two-week dawn-to-dusk shooting schedule was scripted to show-off the cast's acting skills on the golf course, tennis courts and the beach, as well as scenes of them riding in wheelchairs on the Jungle Trail. Munn's male co-stars were David Calhoun with James R. Hyde, the hero, and Roger Hill, the villain, vying for her affection whether dancing in the Cocoanut Grove, flying over the fishing pier or aboard a houseboat on Lake Worth.

Above. The *Palm Beach Girl* film poster. *Library of Congress.*

The Bridal Table in "The Island of Happiness," Palm Beach Fla.

Above. The Royal Poinciana Hotel served as the backdrop for the bridal-table scene in the film *The Island of Happiness.* Shot entirely on Palm Beach, the 1916 society motion-picture starred Marie Louise Wanamaker Munn. *Historical Society of Palm Beach County.*

Below Left. The daughter of Lewis Rodman and Fernanda Wanamaker, Marie Louise Wanamaker married Gurnee Munn who as a child had lived next door to the Wanamakers on Washington's Scott Circle. *Private Collection.*

Hyde and Hill, both aviators, make numerous attempts to win her heart. Hill flies Munn into the Everglades to a place called "No Man's Land." There, she eats berries and shrieks at the sight of a snake. She flees from her abductor into the arms of her hero who hears her screams. After a fistfight, Hyde takes her back to Palm Beach by boat.

In supporting roles, "a bevy of popular girls and young men" participated, including Louise Wise, Mary Lily Flagler's niece, Pittsburgh debutante Ethel Shields, Pauline Disston, who would marry John Wanamaker Jr. in August 1917, Mary Brown Wanamaker Warburton, and Mary Snyder. Unfortunately, everyone involved in the project had agreed "… this film will not be shown outside of Palm Beach, and following its showing, the film is to be burned in the presence of the society artists participating."

However, because of the film's success and reviews, "… the technical work was first class and the acting was finished," another photoplay was scripted and planned for the following season. But this time, the participants approved a wider distribution that would benefit the Ambulance Corps.

The Isle of Tomorrow

In March 1917, much the same ensemble gathered to give an encore performance in *The Isle of Tomorrow*, a film with a more elaborate and complex plot, again directed by Pearl White. The men flew their own planes, raced their private speedboats on Lake Worth, and chased each other along the Ocean Boulevard and Palm Beach Avenue. For this farcical less serious romp, Flo Ziegfeld loaned many of the costumes.

John Rutherfurd, of Tuxedo Park, played the hero. Natalie Johnson, cast as the heroine, was knocked out when she was hit by a golf ball. Unconscious, a lecher who lives at Whitehall, played by Le Grand Cannon, kidnaps her in his aquaplane, and flies down to the shipwreck on the beach in front of The Wigwam, Richard and Beulah Croker's estate south of Widener's Curve. Cannon makes plans to elope with Johnson. Along the way, the film depicts a children's costume party, a dinner party with exhibition dancers in the Cocoanut Grove, and a wedding inside Poinciana Chapel.

Roger Hill played a comic tramp. The heroine's father was played by debonair bachelor and New York stock broker E. Clarence Jones, who two years later became the Everglades Club's first vice-president. Marjorie

Merriweather Post, Mrs. Edward Bennett Close at the time, was Johnson's mother; her aunt was portrayed by Tessie Oelrichs. The heroine's cousins were enacted by Rosamond Lancaster and Mary Brown Wanamaker Warburton.

After the film played to more than a thousand guests in the Royal Poinciana Hotel's new dining room, it was shown at the Bijou theater in West Palm Beach before being nationally distributed by the Pathé-Freres film company. According to their agreement, Pathé-Fréres kept twenty percent of the ticket sales with eighty percent going to the American Ambulance Field Service Corps in France. The following month, the United States entered the war, sending more than one million doughboys to fight in Europe.

Palm Beach became a popular backdrop for some of the era's silent pictures. Society families reveled in documenting their activities with their own movie cameras. Nonetheless, there were never again anything like the films *The Island of Happiness* and *The Isle of Tomorrow*, when society was given the chance of seeing themselves as others see them.

The Isle Of Tomorrow

SOCIETY MOVIES of PALM BEACH LIFE

Showing Thrilling Motor Boat, Auto and Aeroplane Races, Children's Costume Party, Tea Dance in Cocoanut Grove and other familiar scenes at The Millionaires' Playground

May Be Seen at The

BIJOU THEATRE

Above. The Isle of Tomorrow, newspaper advertisement. Silent film star Pearl White directed *The Island of Happiness* and *Isle of Tomorrow*, appearing in each film's prelude "writing an admission that the entire production had been made in the spirit of play." *Palm Beach Daily News archive*.

WILL YOU COME TO A

SEVEN-THIRTY-TO-ELEVEN SQUARE DANCE PRACTICE

AT MAR-A-LAGO

ON *Thursday, February 27*

MARJORIE POST

7:30 COCKTAILS
8:00 BUFFET SUPPER
9:00 WE SQUARE OFF
11:00 "HOME SWEET HOME"

R. S. V. P.
MAR-A-LAGO
1100 SOUTH OCEAN BOULEVARD
TELEPHONE: 833-2466

DAYTIME DRESS

Above. For the select few, the season's most coveted social trophy was an invitation to do-si-do at Mar-A-Lago. *Historical Society of Palm Beach.*

Below. One night a week, the square dance caller and the sounds of the fiddler, bass and guitar turned Mar-A-Lago's dance pavilion into a Texas ranch house where plastic and rubber heel caps were issued to each guest to protect the wooden floor. *Historical Society of Palm Beach.*

5

DANCING BY THE SEA

On New Year's Eve 1961 at Palm Beach, President John F. Kennedy sent holiday greetings to Soviet Premier Nikita Khrushchev. Moments later, the president and first lady arrived at Charles and Jayne Wrightsman's black-tie dinner dance, where Lester Lanin's orchestra might have been playing "Midnight in Moscow" to a crowded dance floor. As much as this formal glamorous event and dance-card cotillions represent the picturesque ideal many have of Palm Beach nightlife, musical tastes were more basic for more down-to-earth residents. Square dance nights at Mar-A-Lago were a popular diversion.

"What a joy it was to see you bouncing around … I am amazed to learn from your letter that it was the first time you ever square danced," wrote hostess Marjorie Merriweather Post in a 1965 note to Rose Kennedy, the president's mother. The note was referenced in Estella M. Chung's book, *Living Artfully: At Home with Marjorie Merriweather Post*. "I have not had so many attractive dancing partners since I was a debutante," the Kennedy matriarch responded – and she became a regular at Post's square dances, which were by then a Palm Beach institution.

Having popularized these folksy get-togethers at her Washington estate's Russian-themed pavilion, Post introduced her square-dance nights to Palm Beach during the 1956 season, when the dance became hotter than the mambo. Post flew-in Maurice Flowers, Washington's best-known and most popular square-dance caller, to emcee at Mar-A-Lago. Even the trendiest, most class-conscious Palm Beachers were seen boxing the gnat, slipping the clutch and shooting the star before Post's mandatory "Lights out!" at 11 p.m. when guests were asked to sashay away.

Square dancing became the vogue. For a barn dance at the Everglades Club, guests wore overalls and prairie skirts with petticoats. Sailfish Club members staged what was billed as a Chuckwagon Party. At the Palm Beach Polo Club, live chickens and cows were brought in to give the dancers a more authentic farmyard atmosphere.

Step by step

From the eagle rock to the twist, Palm Beachers of all ages have long been spellbound by the allure of dancing cheek-to-cheek, whether at The Breakers beneath ballroom chandeliers during a gala or at Nick and Johnnie's, rockin' and rollin' around the dance floor under a million stars. No wonder "dinner dance" is a phrase one encountered again and again on the island's charity-event calendar each season. Throughout the decades, chroniclers in the local press have rarely missed a chance to describe Palm Beachers' fondness for shaking a well-heeled leg.

After the turn of the last century at dinner at Whitehall, Henry and Mary Lily Flagler's own winter palace, guests danced the Virginia reel in a Louis XV gilded ballroom lit by bronze sconces and chandeliers with Baccarat crystals, described, according to an account of the legendary 1903 Bal de Podré, as "a profusion of brightness, velvet shadows and flashing jewels."

Next door at Flagler's Royal Poinciana Hotel, once the afternoon's informal tea dance had ended and dinner and cigars were served, guests could foxtrot in the octagonal ballroom. Or they could turn-and-twirl al fresco in the Cocoanut Grove, where multi-colored lights twinkled between the tree branches. For the more dashing and the debonair, The Breakers orchestra at the Danse La Mer was known to entrance couples until "the sun was ready to bid them good morning."

For those who arrived in 1920s Palm Beach weak-kneed or without knowing the quick-step from the Charleston, Red Thompson and Grace Mills advertised lessons for two dollars per hour in the waltz, foxtrot and tango. On South Ocean Boulevard during rhumba night at Concha Marina, thoughtful hostess Isabel Dodge Sloane provided guests with professional dance instructors to give her guests added confidence.

Above. Henry and Mary Lily Flagler's ballroom at Whitehall introduced a new chapter in the history of Palm Beach at-home entertainment. *Library of Congress*

Above. During the 1938 season, popular conductor John Phillip Sousa III and the Whitehall Orchestra kept an SRO crowd on the dance floor. *Historical Society of Palm Beach.*

Above. Beauty arbiter Estee Lauder and North Lake Way personality Douglas Fairbanks Jr.
take a spin at a charity event. *Palm Beach Daily News file photo.*

At The Breakers, dance host C.C. Roberto had made "a study of reigning dances in important European capitals." In Paris, London and Rome, Roberto declared that "the Viennese Waltz has replaced last season's Rhumba and Tango, though they still enjoy widespread appeal." To add his own personal touch, Roberto acquainted Palm Beach with the Parisian Ballroom Tango, his adaptation of the Argentine Tango.

Shall we dance?

While dance bands and New York orchestras took Palm Beach by storm during the 1920s – when a ballroom was a desirous accessory in many an extravagant home – the resort's succeeding 1930s nightclub era further enhanced the resort's laissez-faire let-loose reputation.

On North Lake Trail at the chic Colony Club, "where sedateness is checked at the door in keeping with the best traditions of the resort," patrons were mad for the Lindy hop, the jive and the jitterbug. At the nearby popular Patio on South County Road, in 1934 owner Sam Salvin offered weekly wrestling matches staged in the middle of the dance floor. But excited as patrons became during these choreographed throw-downs, themed dance parties prevailed. For the nightclub's annual barn dance, café society sophisticates dressed as farmhands, plowboys, peasants, and milkmaids. Hay bales and cornstalks lined the open-air club along with coops filled with live chickens, ducks and turkeys, as Mort Dennis and his society orchestra kept the crowd dancing the Old Dan Tucker.

For Mr. Palm Beach, the late Charles Munn, what set Palm Beach apart from the rest of the world were his memories of dancing until sunrise to the sounds of Flo Ziegfeld's orchestra playing next door on the patio at Louwana, his brother Gurnee Munn's oceanfront estate.

In the ensuing decades, the dancing continued unabated. Longtime Palm Beacher Judy Schrafft recalls a myriad of costumed dance parties as well as Trude Heller's discotheque -- "though we were always home by midnight," she adds, taking note of Palm Beach's dusk-to-dawn playground atmosphere that once made the resort an international destination for partygoers.

Schrafft remembers that the most beautiful place to dance was Thaddeus and Margaret Trout's private ballroom on Barton Avenue.

In 1965, the Trouts added to their ensemble of Midtown properties a small adjacent villa they christened Ballroom House. Designed originally with a forty-five-foot living room for Angier Duke by society architect Addison Mizner, the villa was known as La Colmena when owned for many years by financier and art collector Jules Bache. The Trouts converted the spacious living room into a ballroom. For the next twenty years, they held dinner dances for as many as two hundred of their closest friends.

Long after the last tennis and golf games are played and the final bridge hand has been dealt, memories of candle-lit waltzes in backyard oceanfront tents, moonlight dances in the Orange Garden and midnight bops above the waves on the old Palm Beach Pier enrich Palm Beach's unearthly dimension. It is a place where it is still possible to believe that if you keep moving with the music, the orchestra will never stop.

Above. Palm Beachers Inger and H. Loy Anderson Jr. share a close encounter on the dance floor. *Palm Beach Daily News file photo.*

Above. Although Otto Kahn's North County Road designed by Treanor & Fatio is the property most associated with him, he actually only spent several weeks in the course of two seasons at the Italian Renaissance style mansion before his death in 1934. Addie Kahn and her daughters spent brief seasonal periods before Kahn's estate sold it to the Graham-Eckes School. *Historical Society of Palm Beach County.*

6

OTTO KAHN AT PALM BEACH

From the Gilded Age until the Great Depression, Otto Kahn's stature as a banker, builder and benefactor identified him with New York and London's most influential culture czars. On Palm Beach, however, Kahn never garnered the same social spotlight, although the legendary financier created a considerable architectural legacy, supported many local charities and was a founding member of the town's most exclusive private clubs. Rather than host extravagant soirees or elaborate fundraisers, his wife Adelaide "Addie" Wolff Kahn was known to have guided the architecture and design of her husband's various projects, including the Metropolitan Opera, as well as amassed the couple's considerable art collection. Nonetheless, there could have been a myriad of reasons why the social standing of the German-born British subject who became a naturalized American citizen was overshadowed at the winter resort, where excess and extremes were the standard.

Otto Kahn's counsel and judgment were sought by US presidents, railroad titans and foreign leaders. A popular public speaker, his opinions on world economics and political affairs attracted large audiences. His essays were widely published. Regarded as the nation's greatest arts patron, Otto Kahn transformed the Metropolitan Opera into one of the world's premier stages. At the same time, he also endowed and sustained countless playwrights, actors, artists, dancers, designers, musicians, tenors, and poets. His four-story house at 1100 Fifth Avenue was designated the finest Italian Renaissance mansion in New York by the Landmarks Preservation

Commission. A *New York Times* article described Oheka Castle, his Long Island estate, as "the finest country house in America."

And yet, no matter the compliments and the tributes, Kahn's uncommon mix of downtown savvy and uptown savoir faire was the subject of deprecating anecdotes. He was best known as a partner at Kuhn Loeb & Company, a banking firm considered second to Drexel, Morgan & Co. that lost its cachet when it merged with Lehman Brothers. His Fifth Avenue palace was converted into a parochial school. His Cold Spring Harbor castle is no longer a showplace of splendor. Two of his oceanfront Palm Beach houses were demolished, supplanted by a condominium. Oheka, his North County Road house, came to be better known as Graham-Eckes School. After his death, Kahn's lookalike persona became the iconic symbol for the Monopoly board game that today some associate as Kahn's most enduring accomplishment.

Family matters

Otto Kahn was Jewish, albeit non-practicing. He came from a wealthy cultured family where French and English were studied instead of Hebrew. He married Adelaide "Addie" Wolff, the daughter of Kuhn, Loeb & Company partner Abraham Wolff. The couple shared a passion for art museums, literary salons, operas, and philharmonic concerts rather than attending synagogue. In response to a lifetime of fabricated allegations that Kahn was Episcopalian or Catholic, Kahn once responded: "My parents were not practicing Jews and did not bring me up to be a practicing Jew. But I have never left Judaism and have no idea of doing so." Especially during the last decade of his life, Otto Kahn reaffirmed his Jewish heritage, having become a declared enemy of the Nazi German state during the 1930s.

Before adding Palm Beach to their stationery, the Kahns planned on relocating to Great Britain where there was already an organized movement afoot encouraging Kahn to stand for Parliament. In September 1912, he bought a house in London to accommodate his family of six and fifteen servants. Months later he bought an even larger estate, St. Dunstan's Lodge, situated on fourteen acres in Regent's Park. And then, as the war engulfed Europe, he returned to the United States, opting instead to continue in banking rather than politics and taking steps to become an American citizen.

Upon his return, Kahn donated his London villa to house blind soldiers and sailors. He and his family lived at their East 68th Street residence and Cedar Court, a New Jersey estate, while construction proceeded on a magnificent new palazzo at 1100 Fifth Avenue and a colossal French-styled country house in Cold Spring Harbor. Along with starting plans for a new summer house in Isleboro, Maine, Kahn began a search for a house site at Palm Beach where for the past decade he was a seasonal visitor.

Among the tropical palms

During the 1916 season, Otto Kahn spent several weeks ensconced at Lotus Cottage on the grounds of the Hotel Royal Poinciana. While there, close friend E. Clarence Jones sent Kahn a note with a sketch of a map pinpointing various tracts for sale on Palm Beach. At the same time, prominent Anti-Defamation League lawyer Samuel Untermyer paid $73,000 for a thirty-two acre ocean-to-lake tract south of the Palm Beach Country Club, owned by island pioneer Mel Spenser.

Above Left. Otto Kahn played a key role in developing Palm Beach's social distinction for more than two decades. *Library of Congress.*

Above Right. Adele Wolff Kahn. *Library of Congress.*

A well-known Wall Street stockbroker, Jones, who would later become the Everglades Club's first vice-president, was among the resort's most popular bachelors. Jones had arranged Kahn's membership in the newly built Donald Ross-designed Palm Beach Country Club. Earlier in the year, Kahn coordinated Jones' membership at Long Island's Lido Golf Club. Jones offered to assist Kahn in acquiring any specific Palm Beach property and, if needed, " … will explain locations to you …" After several months of reviewing potential parcels, and having become an American citizen in January 1917, Otto Kahn paid $11,500 for a Midtown oceanfront parcel in Floral Park. The lots extended from Sunset to Sunrise Avenue on both sides of the newly paved Ocean Boulevard, one block from the North Breakers Walk that ran in front of the hotel's cottages.

As Kahn was preparing to build, Phipps family members were already constructing three oceanfront houses in the North End, credited to Vizcaya architect F. Burrall Hoffman Jr. Between two of the Phipps' houses, Villa Artemis and Heamaw, Robert Dun Douglas was building Blythdunes, a Tuscan-style house designed by Miami-based architect H. Hastings Mundy. To the south of El Inca, Michael P. Grace's red-tiled Spanish-style villa later named Los Incas, Eva and E. T. Stotesbury bought a large ocean-to-lake tract they called El Mirasol where two seasons later Addison Mizner would design his first notable Palm Beach residence.

For his Mediterranean style villa at 122 North Ocean Boulevard, Kahn selected architect August Geiger, whose noteworthy Spanish-style Fashion Beaux-Art shopping complex on North Lake Trail opened during the 1917 season. As he began work for Otto Kahn, Geiger shuttled between his offices in Miami and Palm Beach, at work on five houses for Miami's Ocean View Company and remodeling developer Carl Fisher's mansion.

Otto and Addie Kahn meticulously analyzed the architect's plans and cost estimates, having their New York builder and now Palm Beach neighbor E. Clarence Jones suggest revisions. Geiger and Kahn exchanged several letters in August 1917, agreeing on contractor George W. Brown's bid of $32,900 to complete the project. A. A. Jones, a New York decorator, would work with Addie Kahn on the house's interior, whether the ornamental plaster, Corinthian columns, clear cathedral glass, copper basins, or period furnishings.

"Magnificent Home of Otto Kahn nears completion" reported The *Palm Beach Post* in February 1918. Oheka Cottage, as Kahn called it, was located on Sunset Avenue. Guests entered through wrought-iron gates opening onto a spacious courtyard with a gallery supported by Corinthian columns leading into the living room. Detailed with paneled ceilings and walls, the expansive living area overlooked the ocean. The dining room, butler's pantry and kitchen were aligned on the north side; along the southerly street side, Kahn's private office was adjacent to his secretary's office as well as one guest bedroom and bath. A staircase led to "... a large commodious lounge with numerous windows to the east" above the living room, flanked by the Kahns' quarters to the south and four guest bedrooms situated on the north side. A detached structure housed a garage on the ground level with room for a Rolls Royce and three wheelchairs. On the upper story, five servants' rooms were located. However accommodating and spacious, Oheka Cottage did not rival the scale of the Kahns' new Fifth Avenue palazzo or their one-hundred-twenty-seven-room castle on Long Island, or the new greater grandeur that was sweeping Palm Beach.

Above. Designed by architect August Geiger in 1917, the pink-tinted Oheka Cottage at 122 North Ocean Boulevard was Otto and Addie Kahn's oceanfront seasonal residence for fifteen years. *Historical Society of Palm Beach County*.

Oheka Cottage: At Home on Palm Beach

In late February the Kahns arrived at the completed cottage aboard their private rail car with several guests. Among them was Henry Rogers Winthrop, longtime president of the Piping Rock Club. During their first season, they entertained Ned and Eva Stotesbury, several years before Eva Stotesbury ascended as the resort's social arbiter. For decades, Otto Kahn and Eva Stotesbury exchanged letters on topics ranging from her son James Cromwell's latest schemes to her recommendations for a maestro at the Metropolitan Opera that she might have heard in Budapest. Kahn always responded by complimenting her impeccable taste before usually expressing his polite regrets to her requests.

Otto Kahn became a shareholder at Palm Beach Stores on Main Street and County Road, a private co-operative purveyor of high-quality groceries and provisionals for the cottage colony. An avid golfer and fisherman, as well as having a weakness for thousand-dollar chips at Bradley's Beach Club, Kahn also enjoyed real estate speculation, the island's favorite post World War I diversion.

During the next few years, he acquired lots adjacent to his Floral Park property as well as partnered with Palm Beach Estates, a Phipps-family owned company, acquiring several blocks of the Crocker property in the far South End. Kahn indicated interest an acquiring Whitehall but it was snapped up with a $50,000 deposit before he could act. When Paris Singer acquired Gus' Bath and transformed it into the private Palm Beach Swimming Club, he approached Kahn about becoming an investor in the project. For an oceanfront parcel near the Hammon property south of The Breakers, Kahn indicated in a letter to T. T. "Tip" Reese he was ready to accept $125 a front foot after Hiram Hammon had sold for sixty-five dollars a front foot.

Further south along Ocean Boulevard, Kahn bought and sold several large parcels. In 1921, he paid Hubert Krantz $28,000 for 2,650 feet of oceanfront in the Delray Beach and Gulf Stream area, selling it three years later for $39,000. For an ocean-to-lake parcel near Vita Serena, where his friend E. Clarence Jones would build, architect August Geiger sketched a large Italian Renaissance style mansion. After Kahn became a partner, stockholder and property owner in Addison Mizner's Boca Raton magnum opus, he encouraged other investors. "Best tip on the market today, Buy South," said Kahn in a speech shortly before the Mizner folly went bankrupt.

In March 1921, Kahn received several letters from Marion Sims Wyeth. Indicating his interest in working with Kahn, Wyeth sent elevation drawings and floor plans for a Mediterranean-styled villa proposed for the corner of North Ocean Boulevard and Sunrise Avenue adjacent to Oheka Cottage. Wyeth's design was influenced by the patio entrance of the Thomas Hastings house at Westbury and Casa Mia, the eight-bedroom house Wyeth designed for Henry and Adele Seligman on Sunset Avenue for $44,000. Wyeth's plan called for a façade of considerable importance along Sunrise, allowing it to be seen by every car coming down the Ocean Boulevard.

When Kahn requested a terrace along the oceanfront, Wyeth argued that placing a loggia or patio along the eastside was impractical because there was "too much wind on the ocean side and guests would be unable to sit facing the Southeast trade wind … and further, the ocean trail affords no privacy." Because of this disagreement, Kahn selected Bruce Paxton Kitchell, a former Mizner architect, to design Sunrise Villa, a precursor for the much grander Oheka, the house on North County Road that a decade later he would have Treanor & Fatio design.

Kahn spent three weeks at Oheka Cottage during the 1921 season, having arrived aboard his private rail car that slept fourteen. He was assured his staff "provided liquids" for the house in Prohibition-era Palm Beach before his arrival. In February, he was invited to speak at the Palm Beach Rotary Club.

Sunrise Villa

In May 1921, Kahn signed a contract for $40,000 with Brown and Wilcox Company, headed by George W. Brown, who five years earlier built Oheka Cottage. The H-shaped two-story Italian-style villa offered more than six-thousand square feet of living space. By the end of June, the foundation was completed. The twenty-one-by-thirty-one-foot entrance hall featured three large double doors overlooking the ocean. Facing southeast, the seventeen-by-twenty-nine-foot living room featured four large windows overlooking the ocean. In the north wing, the seventeen-by-twenty-one-foot dining room opened onto a large terrace, serviced by a butler's pantry and a breakfast nook for the servants. The second level housed five bedrooms, each with private bath measuring seven-by-ten foot. The five-bedroom servants' quarters were above the detached garage.

With construction nearing completion, Kahn and Kitchell became involved in a dispute about cost overruns. Before he resigned from the job, Kitchell expressed in a letter dated April 22, 1922 that this was "my first experience in which any action of mine as an architect representing the owner has ever been questioned." Despite the friction with Kitchell, Kahn and August Geiger maintained a continued working relationship. Geiger designed several additions to the cottage and had proposed sketches for the elaborate Vizcaya-like estate near E. Clarence Jones' plot at Vita Serena.

Sunrise Villa was completed in early summer and leased to Pennsylvania steel magnate and card sharp J. Leonard Replogle for $7,500 annually. That fall, Leonard and Blanche Replogle bought the house for $135,000. The Replogles added an Italian garden and other improvements, acquiring several parcels to the west along both sides of Sunrise Avenue. A close friend of Flo Ziegfeld, Replogle was best known on Palm Beach as the inventor of Towie, a popular three-handed bridge game.

Above. Sunrise Villa, under construction. *Photograph by Bruce Kitchell*.

Several seasons later, Replogle sold Sunrise Villa for $500,000 to S.W. Straus, chairman of the Ambassador Hotel chain, who had previously leased the oceanfront villa as a beach club for his hotel guests. Situated on a parcel with two hundred and fifty feet of oceanfront, The Colony-Ambassador Beach Club, as it was first named before being called the Sun & Surf Beach Club, finally opened January 15, 1932 after several years of litigation with the Town of Palm Beach. With the addition of tennis courts and more than $800,000 in improvements, this intense activity may have been what caused Kahn to sell Oheka Cottage and relocate to a more private enclave in the North End.

"I have found while at Palm Beach, I literally some days have had scarcely enough time to sit down for a quiet meal during which there are not some interruptions," wrote Kahn, whose seasonal visits to Palm Beach were often reported as recuperative sojourns rather than pleasure excursions. His hectic schedule, however, was of his own making, having opted to plunge into the island's flurry of club life.

Below. Sun & Surf Club, aerial. Otto Kahn was said to have built Sunrise Villa, located adjacent to Oheka Cottage, for his daughters. Upon completion, he sold it to J. Leonard Replogle. Designed by architect Bruce Kitchell, with additions by Treanor & Fatio, the site became the Sun & Surf Beach Club until it was later demolished, along with Oheka Cottage, making room for the Sun and Surf condominium. *Historical Society of Palm Beach County.*

Club class

When Otto and Addie Kahn were listed in the first Palm Beach Social Directory published in 1923, they had already been asked to join the Gulf Stream Golf Club. While there is never any mention of membership in the Everglades Club, where their Sunset Avenue neighbors Henry and Adele Seligman were members, the Kahns subscribed to the Palm Beach Country Club, Oasis Club, Bath & Tennis Club, Seminole Golf Club, Palm Beach Yacht Club, and the Palm Beach Angler's Club, later the Sailfish Club of Florida. Kahn also found time for the Palm Beach Men's Club and the Palm Beach Gridiron Club, only sending regrets to the Palm Beach Press Club.

In November 1925, Anthony "Tony" Drexel Biddle Jr. and Jules Bache enlisted Kahn's financing expertise in acquiring E. R. Bradley's oceanfront parcel and building at the end of Main Street, known then as the Tennis Club property, for $150,000. Along with Biddle and Bache, Kahn was a founding member of the Oasis Club along with W. Forbes Morgan and Henry Rogers Winthrop.

The following summer, Otto Kahn, and Kuhn Loeb partner Mortimer Schiff, were tapped for the board of directors of the Oceanfront Realty Corporation, organized by E. F. Hutton and Tony Biddle. Oceanfront Realty was organized to build a new one-million-dollar Bath & Tennis Club at 1170 South Ocean Boulevard. As one of the club's founding subscribers who each kicked in $10,000, Kahn's perpetual membership was designated Number Seventeen in the club's records. Almost immediately after the club's opening, when the club's first president Tony Biddle increased the board's subscription from $1 million dollars to $1.25 million to cancel current debt, Kahn was among the first members to contribute.

"We are picking our members. We want the cream of Who's Who in America," wrote the president of the Sailfish Club to Otto Kahn, inviting him to join "the most exclusive sports club in the world." Previously, Kahn was a member of the Palm Beach Sports and Anglers Club whose clubhouse on North Lake Trail was taken over by the Sailfish Club of Florida when it merged with several of the island's other fishing clubs. An ardent fisherman, Kahn provided mortgage financing for several of the club's expansions as well as donating the Otto H. Kahn Cup for one of the division winners of an annual sailfish derby. In February 1933, the Sailfish Club extended four life memberships to Kahn's sons, Roger and Gilbert Kahn, and his daughters, Maud Kahn Marriott and Margaret "Nin" Kahn Ryan.

"I have taken two options for shares," wrote Jules Bache to Otto Kahn in February 1929, inviting him to become a founder with proprietary interest in the newly formed Seminole Club. "Ned Hutton's plan is taking shape and I know you will want to be a part of it," continued Bache.

New York, December 28th, 1925.

Otto H. Kahn, Esq.,
52 William St.,
New York, NY

DEC 3 1 1925

Dear Sir:

Believing that the time has come when there is a demand at Palm Beach for a Man's Club, the undersigned Organization Committee have undertaken to complete arrangements for such a club and are sending invitations to a selected number of men to join in the formation of the club.

The Committee has secured for $150,000, 225 feet frontage by 122 feet deep on Main Street extension near the ocean, including a splendid concrete building adaptable to club purposes which probably could not be constructed at present for much less than $100,000. The purchase is made on the basis of $90,000 for the land, viz., $400 per front foot.

It is proposed to take in 250 founder members who will be asked to contribute $1,000 each to cover the purchase of this property and its alteration, and who will ratably own it through shares evidencing their ownership.

The Club will have all the distinctive features of a man's club, viz., reading rooms, card rooms, dining room, etc. It is proposed as soon as possible to build a small annex for bedrooms for visiting members.

While it may not be possible to have the alterations of the building fully completed for the coming season, it is hoped that it will be possible to open the Club for limited use some time in February.

This invitation is being sent to five hundred men, and if you desire to become a Founder Member, kindly sign the enclosed card and return same with your check for $1,000 to the order of Woodward Babcock, Secretary, in the enclosed envelope. Applications will be accepted in the order in which they are received.

Very truly yours,

A. J. DREXEL BIDDLE, JR., *Chairman,*
WOODWARD BABCOCK, *Secretary,*
JULES S. BACHE,
E. CLARENCE JONES,
FREDERIC POTTS MOORE,
W. FORBES MORGAN,
H. R. WINTHROP,
Organization Committee.

Kindly address all communications to
WOODWARD BABCOCK, *Secretary,*
c/o W. FORBES MORGAN,
71 Broadway, New York.

Above. Letter, Oasis Club to Otto Kahn, 1925. *Firestone Library Special Collections, Princeton University.*

BATH AND TENNIS CLUB
PALM BEACH, FLORIDA

December, 1932

To
Founder and Perpetual Members,
BATH AND TENNIS CLUB,
PALM BEACH, FLORIDA:

A Committee of the Governors of the Bath & Tennis
Club was appointed by the President to recommend to the
Governors and Members whether or not the Club should be
opened for the 1933 season,

The Committee has unanimously recommended that the
Club should be opened January 1, 1933. The Committee believes that it might prove impossible to reorganize the
Club after any protracted period of inactivity and in any
event insurance and upkeep expenses must be paid.

The running expenses of the Club have been reduced
from $104,961.52 in 1929 to an estimated $30,000.00 for
the next twelve months. Membership has decreased in the
same period from 253 to about 173, and is almost evenly
divided between Active Dues-paying Members and Perpetual
Founder non-Dues-paying Members.

The dues of the Active Members will be $175.00 for 1933,
plus $17.50 tax, and $175.00 per year for large Cabana rental;
a total expense of $367.50. Perpetual Members pay no dues
but pay Cabana rental if they buy a Cabana for the season.
Founder Members pay neither dues nor Cabana rental.

The financial difficulties of the club are caused by
the fact that half of the membership does not contribute
to its support. It is impossible, during these times, to
add to the expenses borne by the Active Members; the
Governors, therefore, request that the Perpetual and
Founder Members, to whom the Club belongs, each contribute
this year $87.50, or one-half the dues of Active Members,
to support the Club in order that the Club and their investment in it may be saved. Founder Members are further
requested to pay one-half of the regular Cabana dues, if
they use a Cabana during the coming season.

Unless the Perpetual and Founder Members contribute to
the support of the Club the standard of service, which permits the Board of Governors to accept payment by Active
Members of their annual dues, cannot be maintained.

The Committee, judging from available figures, believes
that the Club can be satisfactorily maintained this year,
without any assessment, provided the Founder and Perpetual
Members will co-operate as requested.

THE BOARD OF GOVERNORS
Bath & Tennis Club.

Above. Letter, Bath and Tennis Club, 1932. *Firestone Library Special Collections, Princeton University.*

The following month, Kahn received a formal invitation from Martin Sweeney, the Seminole Club's secretary-treasurer, to be one of the first one-hundred founding members. Kahn not only sent his check for $2,500 but also an additional donation of $2,500 for the club's furnishings.

"Dear Mr. Hutton," wrote Kahn, "I appreciate the fine spirit of your leadership in the creation of the Seminole Club." With a championship Donald Ross golf course and a clubhouse designed by Marion Sims Wyeth, The Seminole Club was regarded one of the nation's most exclusive golf clubs where Kahn and his family entertained on several occasions.

Oheka

After spending fourteen seasons at Oheka Cottage, and his neighbor J. Leonard Replogle having sold Sunrise Villa on the adjacent parcel to be utilized as a beach club, Otto Kahn paid $110,000 to Joseph Speidel for an oceanfront parcel adjacent to Villa Artemis on North County Road. With plans to build an Italian-style mansion designed by Treanor & Fatio, the February 1930 sale was contingent on the closure of North Ocean Boulevard that at the time ran in front of the house separating it from the ocean. Badly damaged during the Hurricane of 1928, property owners from Wells Road to the Palm Beach Country Club were successful in having the road permanently abandoned, after promising to pay for the necessary improvements along North County Road. The month following the special election approving the closure, Kahn bought more land along North County Road to add to his new estate that would now extend one-thousand feet to Lake Worth.

In April 1930, Kahn announced plans for a large-scale $250,000 oceanfront Italian villa with George W. Brown again retained as the contractor. The Treanor & Fatio design called for an expansive living room facing the ocean flanked by Kahn's office to the north and card room to the south. The formal dining room was off the hall leading from the foyer, opening onto the courtyard fountain. For the interiors, Addie Kahn opted for modernistic furnishings by her London designer Curtis Moffett rather than traditional period rooms.

From the beginning, construction at 691 North County Road was beset with problems that might have even rattled a de Medici with whom Kahn was often likened. Because of the abandonment of the ocean road, there were conflicting property lines that postponed seawall building. The contractor's use of dynamite to reform a rock ledge reef led to breaking windows and damaging Villa Artemis, causing the owners to file a civil suit against Kahn and the Town Council to issue a stop work order.

Twilight at Palm Beach

In a December 1930 letter, Kahn described himself as "so utterly overwhelmed by commitments and demand, distress and suffering ..." As construction neared completion, Otto and Addie Kahn sold Oheka Cottage at 122 North Ocean Boulevard, now next to the Ambassador Sun & Surf Beach Club, to Florida Mogar Realty of Jacksonville for $122,000. The sale included fourteen lots in Floral Park, part of two lots on Sunrise Avenue and riparian rights.

Because of Kahn's declining health, he spent the most part of the 1933 season at Europe's health spas, only enjoying a few weeks at his new house. Shortly after spending six weeks of "rest and relaxation" at Palm Beach, Otto Kahn died of a heart attack on March 29, 1934 while having lunch in a private dining room at his Kuhn, Loeb & Co. office in New York. Temple Emanu-El handled the funeral arrangements for burial at the Cold Spring Harbor Cemetery. Addie and her daughters' families spent a few more seasons at Oheka before Otto Kahn's estate sold the house for $60,000 to the Graham-Eckes School. During the late 1960s, the school relocated, selling to an individual owner who converted the now landmarked mansion into a private residence.

Although the *Palm Beach Daily News* recognized Kahn's passing with a wire service report and a four-line acknowledgment of him as a seasonal visitor, *The Palm Beach Post* highlighted his death with a front page headline and an editorial, stating: "Mr. Kahn and members of his family became attached to Palm Beach, always being held in the highest esteem ... Otto H. Kahn, although of foreign birth, ranks with latter day builders of the Republic whose influence will endure."

For more than three decades, Otto Kahn was one of the town's most enthusiastic and dedicated boosters. Among the town's most generous philanthropists, he was as supportive of the efforts of the local Palm Beach Art League as he was the activities of the Palm Beach Shrine Club. Far from Wall Street boardrooms, Kahn enjoyed the camaraderie of golf course foursomes and the company of his fishing companions more so than the frolic of a cakewalk. Dressed in his Saville Row suits, he reveled in his daily walks, tipping his hat along the seaside boardwalk at The Breakers beach. He took pleasure at a white glove tea with Ned and Eva Stotesbury, to whom he expressed, "My admiration for the grace, dignity, aesthetic feeling, and perfect taste of El Mirasol."

"Of all the properties, Palm Beach was Otto's favorite — the place like no other where he could most be himself," said the late John Barry Ryan III, Kahn's grandson, according to Theresa M. Collins, author of *Otto Kahn: Art, Money and Modern Time*. Otto Kahn had unearthed Palm Beach's magic, a world where he was appreciated for simply being himself.

Above. Oheka Cottage, 122 North Ocean Boulevard. Jane Sanford, Otto Kahn, Margaret "Nin" Kahn Ryan, Betty Bonstetton, Nancy Yuille, and Maurice Fatio. *Ellen Glendinning Ordway Collection.*

130 West 57th Street
New York

Villa les Rochers
St. Jean Cap Ferrat

Paris Singer
Architect - Engineer

57 Cadogan Square
London SW

3 Place des Vosges
Paris

TOUCHSTONE WAR WORK

TOUCHSTONE CONVALESCENTS' CLUB, PALM BEACH, FLA. ADDISON MIZNER, ARCHITECT

Above. Paris Singer, calling card, 1920-1925. *Singer family*

Below. Architect Addison Mizner's earliest known sketch for the proposed Touchstone War Work's clubhouse appeared in the Singer-owned Touchstone magazine in August, 1918. *Touchstone, August, 1918.*

7

REMAKING HISTORY

PARIS SINGER &
THE EVERGLADES CLUB

Palm Beach attracts bigger-than-life characters who often prefer their life stories fictionalized by Hollywood's romantic comedies rather than told in unauthorized biographies. Some personalities are so extensively written about, it's assumed everything there is to know about them is already common knowledge. Among them was Paris Singer, founder and builder of the Everglades Club. Considering resort life was intended as an escape from reality, filtering fact from fiction about someone as brilliant and dynamic as Singer can be a daunting task, especially when historians must rely on revised memoirs, decades-old memories, feuds, hearsay, and social columns.

In documenting Paris Singer's real estate ventures at Palm Beach, contemporaneous newspaper reports and records offer only a fragmented timeline. The *Palm Beach Daily News* stopped daily publication for the 1918 season during the last week of March, just as Singer was acquiring sites for his convalescent facility for shell-shocked soldiers. There is no mention of Paris Singer or Addison Mizner in the *Palm Beach Daily News* published from January until March 1918. The March issues of *The Palm Beach Post* that would have reported Singer's first real estate acquisitions are not part of any accessible archive. Thus, at present, a narrative must rely on available court records and the series of articles published in *The Post* during the first week of April 1918, referring to Singer's purchases.

Both historian Donald Curl, author of *Mizner's Florida* (1984), and John R. A. Wilson, author of *Paris Singer: A Life Portrait* (1997), were unable to access documents from and about Paris Singer now available to researchers online at The Smithsonian's American Arts Archive. The Smithsonian's Mary Fanton Roberts Papers collection enhances and expands, as well as contradicts, our knowledge of Paris Singer and the building of the Everglades Club. These previously unpublished resources include handwritten and typed letters and telegrams from Paris Singer, Joan Bates Singer and Singer's son, Cecil Singer. They were postmarked Palm Beach, New York, London, Paris, and St. Jean, Cap Ferrat.

Because Paris Singer died unexpectedly at a relatively young age, various recollections of his life became secondary subject matter for other people's biographies, which were inclined to portray him as an impulsive martinet or a well-mannered autocrat. These characterizations resulted in a romanticized version of events, whether by an Isadora Duncan selectively recalling what she perceived was her relationship with Singer or anecdotal narratives recounting Singer's last hurrah on Palm Beach. Added to these inconsistent characterizations were the expectations Singer faced having to reconcile his own complex persona with his father's scandalous personal life.

Paris Singer & the Singer Family

The Singer family's patriarch, Isaac Merritt Singer (1811-1875), was as well-known for fathering numerous children, both legitimate and out of wedlock, as being the founder of the Singer Manufacturing Company, which had sold six million sewing machines by the 1870s. Isaac Singer's immense wealth may have shielded his laissez-faire lifestyle from having to adhere to the era's strict moral standards, but his lawless relationships resulted in a tangled will contest over his $15 million estate between his two wives, three mistresses and twenty-four children.

The subsequent settlement significantly affected Paris Singer's future. In 1879, a probate court ruled that Paris Singer's mother, Isabella Eugenie Boyer Singer, was the legal widow. That made her six children — Adam Mortimer, Winnaretta, Washington, Isabelle Blanche, Franklin, and Paris — the estate's richest heirs. The remaining offspring made due with considerably less. By age eighteen Singer's weekly income was reported to

Above. Paris Singer (1867-1932). Described at the time of his death as one of the most important figures in the history of Palm Beach, Singer's local legacy was tainted when the crash of his real estate developments threatened the Everglades Club's financial future. *Historical Society of Palm Beach County.*

Above. Everglades Club, original façade. 1919. Pen and ink sketch. This sketch of the Everglades Club's original façade became a familiar sight at the top of *The Palm Beach Post*'s social page.

Center. A view of the Everglades Club before the extensive 1925 additions changed the building's Worth Avenue façade. *Historical Society of Palm Beach County.*

Below. Addison Mizner's sketch depicts Worth Avenue before the villas were built west of the clubhouse. *Touchstone, September 1918.*

be $15,000, enabling the budding impresario's diverse interests in the arts, medicine, architecture, and engineering. In addition to Singer's studies at Caius College, Cambridge, Singer was believed to have studied architecture and engineering in Paris.

> During his early twenties Paris Singer found time to study architecture, probably at the fashionable Ecole des Beaux Arts in Paris, and obtained a degree, though he assumed the role of patron rather than practitioner in later life. Nevertheless, he is recorded as the architect of No. 3 Cadogan Gate, the large annex behind his mansion on London's Sloane Street, which apparently bore a brass plate engraved 'P. E. Singer – Architect' on the mews entrance door about 1900. *Paris Singer: A Life Portrait.* John R. A. Wilson. Torquay Library.

Although there are mentions of Singer as an architect-engineer in England and France, he became best known for transforming the family's estate called The Wigwam into an elaborate one-hundred room mansion modeled on Versailles. Having bought out his brothers' interest in The Wigwam, Singer renamed it Oldway House. Upon the addition of an elaborate theater and ballroom, Singer presented a performance of Gounod's Faust with singers and settings from the Paris Opera.

When he wasn't supporting the arts or registering numerous mechanical engineering patents, Paris Singer organized utility and transportation companies, including the City and Suburban Electric Carriage Company. He invested in Rudolph Diesel's engines and other similar inventions. Singer also provided support for Eugéne-Louis Doyen, a French surgeon who became known for introducing photography and film into the operating room. At one point, Singer attempted to establish a research institute in Paris. Because nearby property owners overwhelmingly opposed it, the institute was never realized.

Being the son of one of the world's wealthiest and most influential inventors and heir to a considerable fortune, Paris Singer was accustomed to having his tangled private life heralded on the front pages of French and English broad sheets. He and his first wife, Cecilia "Lily" Graham Singer, were married in October 1887 in Hobart, Tasmania. Their four children were Herbert George, Cecil Graham, Paris Graham, and Winnaretta. By

1910, Paris and Lily remained married although they were no longer living together, according to court documents filed during their later divorce.

From his affair with dancer Isadora Duncan, Singer fathered a child named Patrick. While their affair was said to be over soon after their son was born, Singer continued to support Duncan and his child even though he had already begun a liaison with Joan Bates. Singer's son by Duncan died in 1913 from the most unfortunate of accidents. By the following year, Singer and Joan Bates were living together in London, Paris and New York. Legally divorced in December 1918, Bates became the second Mrs. Paris Singer the following year in New York.

As World War I consumed Europe, Singer had settled in New York, becoming an American citizen. He was engaged in real estate as well as the arts. He was the principal patron of Mary Fanton Roberts' magazine The Touchstone, formerly known as The Craftsman. In March 1917, Singer came to Palm Beach and bought a cottage on Peruvian Avenue. The following year he returned to his Palm Beach cottage accompanied by architect Addison Mizner. It was then that Singer bought a seventy-acre tract of undeveloped property on Lake Worth with plans to build a convalescent facility for shell-shocked soldiers.

Paris Singer at Palm Beach

By the time Paris Singer arrived on Palm Beach, the Singer family's triumphs and transgressions had been headline news for more than sixty years. Stories recounting the sewing machine heir's Palm Beach chapter usually begin with a weary Paris Singer and a distressed Addison Mizner arriving as invalids waiting to die of social ennui. The mismatched odd couple's fabled tale always includes a nurse, who happened in reality to be Joan Bates, Singer's longtime mistress who at one time was also his nurse. Bates shuttled between New York, England and France, overseeing Singer's properties that functioned as hospitals. The Singer-Bates-Mizner threesome legend was a fabled twist on the actual series of events when Mizner fell ill while recovering from a leg injury at Singer's villa on Peruvian Avenue. In a letter to Mary Fanton Roberts, the editor of the Singer-owned Touchstone Magazine, a robust energetic Paris Singer appears to refute details of the more popular story:

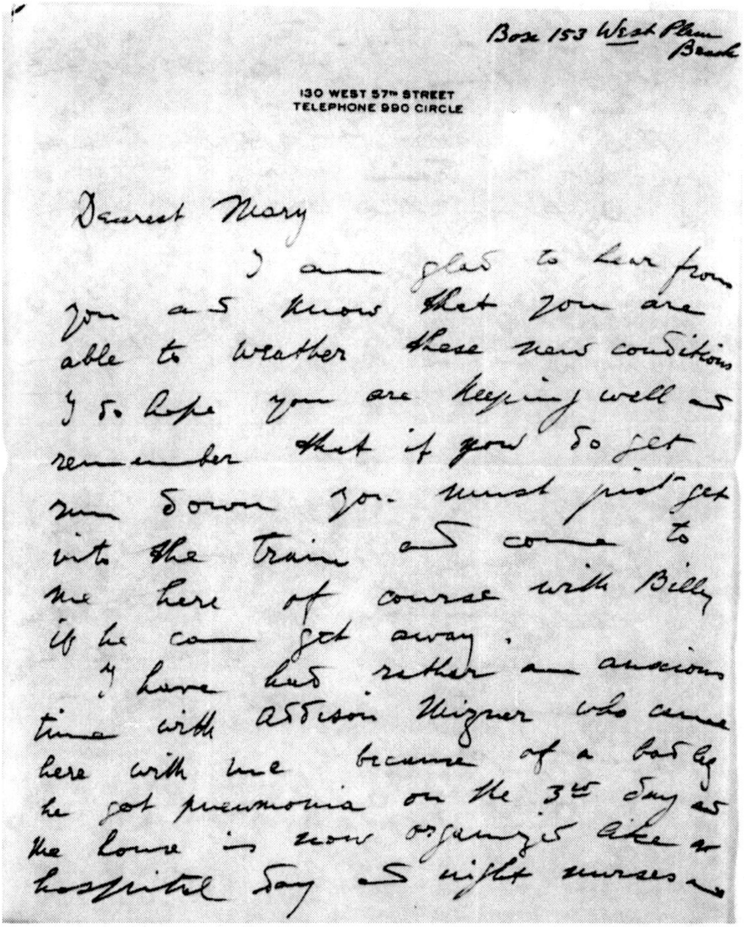

Box 153 West Palm Beach

130 WEST 57TH STREET
TELEPHONE 990 CIRCLE

Dearest Mary

I am glad to hear from you and know that you are able to weather these new conditions I do hope you are keeping well and remember that if you do get run down you must just get into the train and come to me here of course with Billy if he can get away.

I have had rather an anxious time with Addison Mizner who came here with me because of a bad leg he got pneumonia on the 3rd day and the house is now organized like a hospital day and night nurses and

Dearest Mary … I have but rather a time with Addison Mizner who came here with me because of a bad leg. He got pneumonia on the third day of his visit and the house is now organized like a hospital, day and night with nurses and a doctor twice a day. The weather here is all for him and he is now out of danger but it was touch and go. There are very few people here so far but the trains seem to come in as before the war with dining cars, etc. … A man coming here to see Mizner the other day says he talked to Isadora in Washington? Is she back in the East again?

Above. Letter, Paris Singer to Mary Fanton Roberts. *Archive of American Arts, Smithsonian*.

Above. Everglades Club, Venetian terrace. *Historical Society of Palm Beach County.*

Below. Everglades Club villas, aerial. The Addison Mizner-designed villas were originally painted in array of colors, including pale blue, pale green, warm orange, a plain white, and a warmer blue. The villa roofs were described as "red, but not too red, tile roof, weather-worn and studiously irregular." *Historical Society of Palm Beach County.*

During the weeks Paris Singer began buying property to build his convalescent facility on Worth Avenue, Palm Beach residents were waking up to the latest World War I headlines and the results from golf rounds and tennis sets. Along with staging various benefits to aid the war effort, the local social set, led by Tessie Oelrichs and Eva Stotesbury, was raising funds to establish Good Samaritan Hospital, the area's first major medical facility.

Building the Everglades Club

On March 31, 1918, *The Palm Beach Post* reported Paris Singer's real estate plans in a front page story. At the same time American soldiers were joining the Allies in the war against Germany, Singer had spent $250,000 on eight adjacent parcels located in Palm Beach's Royal Park subdivision. With his architect Addison Mizner and lawyer Jerome Wideman, Singer incorporated a holding company to manage, develop and build on his latest acquisition. The following day, a local social columnist mentioned that Paris Singer and his architect, Addison Mizner, had returned to Palm Beach following a four-day weekend in Miami where they were guests at Vizcaya, the James Deering estate. Upon his return, Singer announced his Palm Beach clubhouse would be built in the Old World style, as if it had always been there, much like Vizcaya.

Several years before Singer conceived of the club, Vizcaya architect F. Burrall Hoffman Jr. had designed Palm Beach's first oceanfront mansions for the Phipps family. In Miami, Hoffman's project for Deering was five years in the making, The July 1917 issue of *The Architectural Review* was dedicated to Vizcaya. By the time, Singer and Mizner began planning the facility's main clubhouse, Vizcaya had already received considerable architectural acclaim. Two weeks before Singer and Mizner's jaunt to Vizcaya, Deering was in Palm Beach visiting designer Paul Chalfin, who then operated a studio on North Lake Trail aboard a houseboat tied up at the Beaux Arts docks.

However much the original clubhouse's aesthetic mix visually contrasts with the Deering villa's more formally-modeled Renaissance elevations inspired by Villa Rezzonico, both the Everglades Club and Vizcaya were comprised of much the same ensembles of courtyards, loggias, and arcades. In his original L-shaped plan for the Touchstone Convalescent Hospital,

Mizner included a Venetian Landing outfitted with gondolas along the club's lakefront, akin to Vizcaya's bayfront ambiance. Contemporaneous news reports first described the clubhouse as a fusion of Spanish and Italian features. The club's original Worth Avenue façade is unmistakably similar to Vizcaya's north elevation. However much the Everglades Club has long been regarded a stylistic departure from Palm Beach's existing landscape, in addition to its architectural debt to Vizcaya, the club's original composition was actually harmonious with the era's emerging preference for Italian and Spanish architecture.

By the time Singer and Mizner announced their plans, several noticeable red-tiled roofs and stucco arches were already scattered around the resort. North of Henry C. Phipps' Heamaw and Michael Grace's El Inca, both initially described as Spanish with red-tiled roofs, Miami architect Harold Hastings Mundy had already finished Blythdunes, a Tuscan-styled oceanfront house for Robert Dun Douglass. In 1917, developer Stanley Warrick opened the doors to the often overlooked and under-appreciated Spanish-styled Beaux Arts Fashion Building & Promenade on North Lake Trail that was designed by architect August Geiger. Having established a Miami office in 1910, Geiger is widely credited with introducing the Spanish style to South Florida, adding a Palm Beach office in 1915. In Midtown's Poinciana Park, J. B. Elwell was residing in a Moorish-styled lakeside mansion on Seabreeze Avenue. An Italian villa was under construction on South Ocean Boulevard Clearly, the Everglades clubhouse was conceived as much to blend in with an array of existing buildings at Palm Beach as it was inspired by Vizcaya, the area's most renowned architectural landmark since Henry Flagler built Whitehall.

Several days after the first announcement, Paris Singer and Addison Mizner returned to New York where they unveiled plans to build ten large villas for shell-shocked soldiers along the lakefront in Palm Beach. In addition, Singer bought six-hundred-sixty feet of oceanfront land contiguous with his present holdings, expanding the easterly extent of his parcels from the Atlantic Ocean to Lake Worth. To the south, he bought the offshore island across from his Worth Avenue site. "New York Millionaire buys Cabbage Island" read a local headline.

During the following weeks that Singer and Mizner were ensconced at the Ritz-Carlton Hotel in New York, there were almost daily stories about his plans for Palm Beach. With four sons fighting in the war, erecting the convalescent hospital would convey Singer's sense of philanthropy and patriotism. In Great Britain, Singer's Oldway mansion was already converted into a six-hundred-bed Red Cross hospital. His London house became a sixty-room hospital. Singer's maison de ville in Paris was refitted as a fifty-bed hospital. Les Rochers, the Singer villa on the French Riviera, was also being utilized as a military facility.

Above. Everglades Club, original façade. 1919. *Historical Society of Palm Beach County.*

Above. Everglades Club, staircase. *Library of Congress.*

At Palm Beach, where everything would be Italian or Spanish architecture, or a combination of the two, Singer said his ten villas would be turned over to the government for free as long as they were utilized to aid the recovery of wounded officers. The Continental villas were for the wounded from England and France. The Palm Beach villas would accommodate returning American soldiers. These two sets of villas would be built along the Worth Avenue lakefront, located on nineteen lots in Royal Park, bounded on the south and west by Lake Drive, by Cocoanut Row on the east, and Peruvian Avenue to the north.

For Cabbage Island, Singer envisioned a miniature Venice, inspired by what he had seen at Vizcaya. Cabbage Island would be subdivided into six separate islands connected much like Venice. To the south of the Convalescent Colony, the existing jungle would be developed as a park with trails and a lakefront restaurant. In an obvious reference to Flagler's Whitehall, Singer declared, "There will be no big white houses with glaring red roofs." He would not build "something laid out with a yardstick," but instead, "... something that looks old, like it has always been there, with soft colors."

In early May 1918, Singer returned to Palm Beach, again accompanied by Addison Mizner, to start work on the proposed Touchstone War Work, as the project was also called. Local newspaper stories described Mizner as being associated with "some of the most attractive buildings in America." The partners opened an office on Gardenia Street in West Palm Beach, opposite the Lainhart and Potter Lumber Company, where they placed orders for the project's construction materials. Singer announced his lakefront refuge would accommodate "only such men in need of the invigorating influences of this climate." Dr. Sherman Downs, of Saratoga Springs and the former physician at The Breakers, was named the resident physician who would prescribe treatments for the soldiers. Touchstone magazine sponsored a national program called the "Back to Health Movement for our Wounded Men." Having spent the past two winters at Palm Beach, Singer stated, "Lake Worth is studded with islands and the scenery is beyond words, beautiful. The soldiers' recovery will be stimulated by deep-sea fishing, wild pig hunting, alligator hunting, and wild duck shooting."

During the early summer of 1918, Singer sent a telegram to Touchstone magazine editor Mary Fanton Roberts saying, "... Mizner does interesting picture of club. Would make good magazine cover in Fall. Sending it. Love, Paris." The magazine published Mizner's earliest known sketch for the club's waterfront elevation that looked inspired by, if not borrowed from, Vizcaya's bay-front façade. Further, the magazine announced classes would be offered to women in New York who wanted to be useful companions to the veterans in Palm Beach. It was during that summer when Singer detailed more of his plans. He told a reporter that he spent millions as a "loving donation to the cause of democracy," describing his efforts as non-profit, patriotic, and humanitarian. In the same article, Singer described Mizner as "the well-known and genial New York architect who is now staying in Palm Beach all the time to devote to this project."

With the greenhouses, gardens and villas already underway, construction would soon begin on a palatial clubhouse for the soldiers and sailors. A dredge was digging a basin on the club's lakefront. Tunisian tiles were stored in a warehouse in West Palm Beach. Mizner explained, "Tunis was the Palm Beach of its day." Five greenhouses housed thousands of crotons being rooted. Singer purchased a nearby farm to supply the facility with fresh dairy products and produce.

In August, Singer's altruistic venture was halted by a labor dispute. Construction workers led a strike, demanding Singer pay them at least what was considered minimum wage. Singer argued that patriotic carpenters should return to work or he would move the entire project to California. The local Labor Council gave in to his argument that The Touchstone War Work was a patriotic undertaking and agreed to exempt the Singer project. Singer responded by acquiring more property – this time in West Palm Beach, where the Gables Hotel would house sixty French widows and their children. Singer said the widows would help nurse the wounded men.

By autumn, the project consisted of eight completed villas. The Clubhouse foundation was laid facing Worth Avenue to serve as a gateway to the jungle beyond. Semi-tropical in style, Singer reiterated that the clubhouse was being built not to furnish hospital rooms and treatment but as a place for men already discharged from hospitals who needed peace and calm in their lives. To the south of the greenhouses, the alligator pens remained, the last vestiges of Alligator Joe's tourist attraction. In order to express the project's focus on sportsmanlike therapy, The Touchstone was renamed the Everglades Rod and Gun Club.

Above. Everglades Club, Marble patio loggia. *State Archives of Florida.*

Below. First named the Court of Orange Blossoms before being renamed the Court of Oranges, this open-air courtyard was the club's first breakfast room. After a seawall was built, the gardens extending from the Venetian Terrace to the lake were named the Orange Gardens and the courtyard became the Marble Patio. *Library of Congress.*

The club's dinner deluxe evenings offered grapefruit cocktail, Portuguese filet of striped bass, Colbert medallions of beef bouquetiere, salade Everglades, Meringue glace Chantilly, and Café with special petits fours.

*Above.*Everglades Club, Armada dining room. *State Archives of Florida.*

The main clubhouse would be furnished with Old World treasures from Paris Singer's collection. The club's two-thousand-year-old Tunisian tile was said to be from ancient Troy that the mythological Helen may have walked on. The club's four-hundred-year-old doors would be carved with the heads of saints. To better appreciate the level of the Singer endeavor, Mizner staged an exhibit of rare furniture pieces at Speer Pharmacy on Clematis Street in West Palm Beach.

As Germany was surrendering and accepting the terms for the armistice, Touchstone magazine featured another set of watercolor illustrations of the "First Shell-Shock Club in America for Soldiers and Sailors." The villas were painted pale blue, pale green, warm orange, a plain white, and a warmer blue. They were roofed with red – but not too red -- tile, weather-worn, and set in irregular patterns. The clubhouse was described as a harmonious blend of feudal, Medieval, Spanish, and Italian styles.

According to the clubhouse plans, the dining room measured seventy-by-forty-feet and the ceiling reached forty feet from its lowest point to the massive beams. The eighty-five-by-forty-four-foot living room was centered with a fireplace six-and-one-half-feet high, said to be "large enough to roast an ox." Suggesting a residence for barons and monks, the main building also housed a ladies room, cloak rooms, a club office, and musicians' balconies with narrow-arched doorways.

On the clubhouse's east side, the plans included an inner patio named the Court of Oranges, also functioning as a breakfast room; to the west of the living room, a right-angled double-terrace with a lower level forming a true Venetian landing stage overlooking Singer Basin. The tower's two uppermost floors housed apartments for Singer and Mizner. To the west of the tower, twelve bedrooms were aligned on the second level.

With the war ended and his divorce finalized, Paris Singer returned to Palm Beach on December 1. He arrived with the club's newly named secretary, Frederic Roosevelt Scovel. Scovel's mother, Maria Roosevelt Scovel, was a cousin of President Theodore Roosevelt. His father, Edward Scovel, was titled Chevalier by the King of Italy. Although Singer only stayed a few days, within the following weeks, newspaper reports headlined "Palatial homes for shell-shocked convalescent soldiers built by Singer nearing completion." A mid-December article in *The Palm Beach Post* provided a detailed view of the completed project:

> The main clubhouse suggests a castle. The clubhouse utilizes quaint antiquities from Spain and Italy, such as the iron doors at the entrance on Worth Avenue. Upon entering, cloakrooms are located for men and women. The cloak room is the only room provided for women, for this is to be a man's club. Ahead, looking through the building is a view to the south of the Orange Court and to the west to the lake and the island. The lounging room and the dining room are high-ceilinged and paneled. These rooms evoke recollections of Washington Irving's Alhambra or of old English inns. Decorated beams reproduce the period long past. The first floor also includes a model kitchen and servant's quarters. *The Palm Beach Post*.

With the world at peace, it became more apparent Singer's convalescent colony would not become a sanctuary for wounded veterans but a private residential and social club. Although by mid-January, it was still advertised as the "Everglades Club for Convalescent Soldiers: Most Complete of its Kind in the United States," there was a minimal response. Singer had invested one million dollars into the Palm Beach project. Thus, Singer resorted to creating an exclusive residential club where members of the Social Register might recuperate from the stress of metropolitan life. Since the need for wounded officers following the armistice never materialized, the Everglades Club was repurposed as an exclusive club.

The Everglades Club

Even before the club's formal opening, or Singer's own arrival, guests with impeccable social credentials were checking-in rather than shell-shocked soldiers. The dining room seated one-hundred-fifty to two-hundred members and guests. There was a large living room, several reception rooms, and twelve bedrooms and baths for residential members. The seven villas each featured seven bedrooms and living rooms with one of them occupied by the club's resident physician.

By Christmas week, the front of the club was lined with wheelchairs. The Yellow Villa was taken by Mr. and Mrs. Jerome Napoleon Bonaparte; the White Villa by Mrs. Charles B. Alexander and her daughter, Mary

PALM BEACH LIFE

Mr. E. Clarence Jones recently gave a dinner dance at the Everglades Club to about one hundred of his friends, the party being in honor of Mr. Paris Singer. Twined in and out of the tracery of the broad balcony that is an architectural feature of the banquet hall were vivid sprays of orange flame-vine which were most effective against the fine old panelling with its mellow tone of brown. The dinner was served at small tables which were decorated with sweet peas. The guests included Mr. and Mrs. Pierre Lorillard Barbey, Mr. and Mrs. James King Clarke, Mr. and Mrs. Stanley Grafton Mortimer, Mr. and Mrs. Edward T. Stotesbury, Mr. and Mrs. John F. Harris, Mr. and Mrs. Douglas Paige, Mr. and Mrs. Kenneth Van Riper, Mr. and Mrs. William Thaw, 3rd, Mr. and Mrs. Leonard D. Ahl, Mr. and Mrs. Harlan K. Bolton, Mr. and Mrs. Jerome N. Bonaparte, Mr. and Mrs. David Caohoun, Mr. and Mrs. Edward Browning, Mr. and and Mrs. Grafton Pyne, Mr. and Mrs. J. Frederick Pierson, Mrs. Edward Brownin, Mr. and Mrs. Henry McVickar, Mr. Jr., Dr. and Mrs. A. Sherman Downs, Mr. and Mrs. L. Harrison Dulles, Mr. and Mrs. Frank Pierce Frazier, Mr. and Mrs. Frank Duff Frazier, Mr. and Mrs. William Lawrence Green, Mr. and Mrs. Theodore Frothingham, Jr., Mr. and Mrs. Lewis Quentin Jones, Mr. and Mrs. George Kingsland, Mr. and Mrs. F. Roosevelt Scovel, Mr. and Mrs. Leland Sterry, Mr. and Mrs. Theodore Schulze, Mr. and Mrs. William Simons, Mr. and Mrs. Charles E. VanVleck, Jr., Mr. and Mrs. John Rutherfurd, Mr. and Mrs. Artemas Holmes, Mr. and Mrs. C. H. Waring, Mrs. Harry Payne Bingham, Mrs. Herman Oelrichs, Mrs. Frederic Cruger, Mrs. Charles Harding Howell, Miss Dorothy Stone Smith, Miss Harriett McCook, the Misses Betty and Suzanne Pierson, Miss Mary Alexander, and Messrs. John Bradley Kitchen, Joseph B. Elwell, Roger Hill, Henry T. Sloane, Caleb Bragg, Russell G. Colt, Van Duzer Burton, LeGrand Cannon, Addison Mizner, J. Stinson, Paris Singer, and Thomas Hunt Talmadge.

Above. First Everglades Club reception and dinner. *Among the Palms, Palm Beach Life.*

* * * *

Mr. Addison Mizner had about fifty friends for tea at the Everglades Club recently, this being the first big party given at the new club. Mr. Irving Berlin played some of his own compositions and Mrs. D. C. Calhoun sang various selections, to the great pleasure of all who heard them.

* * * *

11 FEBRUARY 1919

ADDISON MIZNER · ARCHITECT

Above. Addison Mizner hosted an afternoon event on the club's opening day, featuring his friend Irving Berlin at the piano. *Among the Palms, Palm Beach Life*.

Below. Addison Mizner's first sketches for the seven villas intended to house French, English and American veterans. *Touchstone, August 1918*

Crocker; and, the Green Villa reserved for Mr. and Mrs. F. Roosevelt Scovel. The membership tallied one-hundred names with new ones being proposed daily. Nelson Slater was the first to occupy the apartment in the Club Tower above Addison Mizner's residence. The club offered a fleet of motor boats, tennis courts and a nearby log cabin, where hunting parties could track down turkey, quail and deer. Three of five proposed motorboats were anchored in the basin with Captain Wilson Rowan in command. A tea dance was scheduled between three and six o'clock every afternoon. A nine-hole golf course would open the following season.

With the Busoni Orchestra from New York booked to arrive in Palm Beach on February 1, 1919, the club's formal opening was scheduled for three days later. Paris Singer, the club's president, was reported to be indisposed in New York and his presence for the opening was still tentative, but the club's other officers would be in attendance. The Everglades Club's inaugural governing body included E. Clarence Jones, vice-president; T. Tipton "Tip" Reese, treasurer; and F. Roosevelt Scovel, secretary. The club's founding board of governors was Pierre Barbey, Harlan Kent Bolton, William Lawrence Green, Lewis Quentin Jones, Frederick P. Moore, E. Clarence Jones, Walter J. Mitchell, Henry C. Phipps, T. Tipton Reese, Paris Singer, Joseph E. Speidel, J. Frederick Pierson, and Edward T. Stotesbury.

Shortly before the opening, Paris Singer arrived in time to host a pre-opening lunch at the Palm Beach Country Club with the club's one hundred charter members and its first honorary member, W. H. Beardsley, president of the Florida East Coast Railway and Hotel Company. As workmen continued with the club's finishing touches, Addison Mizner hosted the first big party at the club on the afternoon of February 4 with Irving Berlin at the piano. That evening, Singer and E. Clarence Jones held a members-only dinner in the club's dining room. With European resorts taking at least another five years to rebuild from the devastation of by World War I, the Everglades Club was almost instantly popular. During the winter season members were elected at weekly board meetings held on Mondays and their names were routinely publicized the following day in the *Palm Beach Daily News* and *The Palm Beach Post*.

The Everglades Club's formal opening made social headlines in Philadelphia, Washington, Chicago, and New York. *The New York Sun* reported the club had one-hundred-twenty-five members, among them,

Reginald Boardman, Charles F. Choate, Richard Croker, Fulton Cutting, James Deering, George Peabody Gardner, and John Rutherfurd. The *New York Tribune* reported, "The largest social affair of the season was the opening of the Everglades Club the other night ... There are fancy canoes, sailboats, fast motor boats, servants with turbans and sashes, and, in fact, every touch known to the stage which the development smacks strongly of. It has cost about a half-million dollars, in addition to the real estate. The handsome new club, erected for the use of French officers, caught fire during a housewarming a few nights ago but the damage was slight. The blaze occurred at dinner time. The diners rushed to the street but returned to finish their meal. A dinner was being given for Mrs. Vernon Booth of Chicago. The guests included Stanley Mortimer, Grafton Pyne, Mrs. Quincy Shaw 2nd, John B. Kitchen, Robert Toland, Mr. and Mrs. John Rutherfurd, and Mr. and Mrs. William Lawrence Green."

The following month, *The Palm Beach Post* featured "Society Leaders at Palm Beach" with a photograph of the club's social arbiters taken inside the Court of the Oranges. The photograph featured Mrs. Walter Mitchell, Mrs. Harlan Bolton, Mrs. Pierre Barbey, Mrs. John F. Harris, Mrs. E. T. Stotesbury, Mrs. Joseph Speidel, Mrs. William Lawrence Green, and Mrs. Lewis Quentin Jones.

By the beginning of March, Paris Singer had returned to New York. The club's popularity grew. At the end of the first nine-week season, there were three hundred annual subscribers and the club's rooms were completely booked with many applications refused because of lack of rooms. New members included: F. Burrall Hoffman Jr., Phillip Stevenson, Marion S. Wyeth, Leonard Thomas, William Gammell, James Byrne, David Forgan, John F. Kelly, and Courtland Field Bishop. The improvements announced to be completed before next season included the golf course and clay tennis courts. The club's second season would be from December 15, 1919 until April 15, 1920. After the club closed, Paris Singer announced he paid $25,000 for the Hotel Arches located on the oceanfront at Australian Avenue, sold two hundred-feet of oceanfront north of Gus' Baths for $45,000, and sold the Gables Hotel to the Elks Club of West Palm Beach.

Because the Everglades Club had three applications for every room, during the summer of 1919 the club added fifteen accommodations along the south side of the club. On the clubhouse's northeast side, three hundred

SINGER—MR. AND MRS. CECIL M. (Laura Groves). Ever-
glades Club. (Absent.)
Perm. Address—"Occombe House," Paignton, England.
Clubs—Everglades, Torbay Country Club (England), Royal
Automobile Club.
College—Trinity, Cambridge.
Children—Winnaretta and Susan.

SINGER—MR. AND MRS. GEORGE (Vera Marguerite Sar-
torius). Everglades Club.
Perm. Address—England.
Club—Everglades.
Children—Paris George Sartorius Singer and Francis Merritt
Singer.

SINGER—MR. MORTIMER M. Everglades.
Perm. Address—60 Avenue Victor Hugo, Paris.
Clubs—Travellers Club (Paris), Polo Club (Paris), Fontaine-
bleau Golf (Paris), Everglades.

SINGER—MR. AND MRS. PARIS (Annie Charlotte Bates).
Everglades Club. Tel. 2-2191.
Perm. Address—1 Bis Place des Vosges and Mes Rochers
St. Jean Ferrat, France, and 21 East 52nd St., New York
City.
(Arriving December.)
Yacht—"Mildred Grace."
Clubs—Oasis, Bath and Tennis, Pres. Everglades, Gulf Stream
Golf, New Oxford and Cambridge, Royal Thames Yacht,
Royal Automobile, Ranleigh Travellers, Automobile Club
de France, Yacht Club de Nice, Players.
College—Caius College, Cambridge, Eng.

The largest social affair of the season was the opening of the Everglades Club the other night ... There are fancy canoes, sailboats, fast motor boats, servants with turbans and sashes, and, in fact, every touch known to the stage which the development smacks strongly of.

Above. Singer family at Palm Beach *Social Register, c. 1920.*

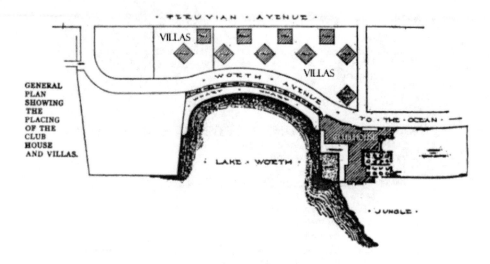

CONVALESCENTS' CLUB FOR SOLDIERS

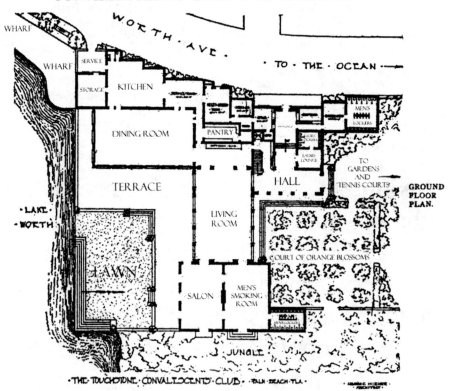

Above & Below. As designed by Addison Mizner, the general plan and floor plan for the Everglades clubhouse and villas. The villas neared completion before construction began on the clubhouse. *Touchstone, August, 1918.*

golf lockers were planned – two hundred for men and one hundred for women. Across the street, a garage was being built to accommodate forty or more cars, with servants' quarters above. To the south of the clubhouse, the old Jungle Trail was being cleared for the golf course designed by Seth Raynor and Charles Blair MacDonald.

As work was being completed for the second season under the supervision of former Piping Rock Club manager R. F. Denzler, Paris Singer and F. Roosevelt Scovel arrived on December 22. New sofas were added to the club's Living Room, gold in color with splashes of mauve and blue flowers. Afternoon tea dances would again be held from four to six p.m. on Wednesdays and Saturdays. Thursday and Sunday nights were reserved for five dollar prix-fixe dinner-deluxe and dancing nights. Thursday evenings were designated Venetian Fete nights, complete with Italian singers and a fleet of gondolas.

On gala nights, dinner was served at 8:30, presented "in true medieval fashion at long tables with gorgeous old tapestries and crimson and gold altar cloths" followed by a supper service at 1 a.m. A menu from one of the club's dinner deluxe evenings offered grapefruit cocktail, Portuguese filet of striped bass, Colbert medallions of beef bouquetiere, salade Everglades, Meringue glace Chantilly, and Café special petits fours. Breakfast was served in the Court of Oranges patio.

When Singer returned to Palm Beach on January 8 for the opening of the second season, he received congratulations on his recent marriage to Joan Bates. The club was already near capacity, having added a Ladies Association annual membership. Because of the club's tremendous popularity, board meetings were now held every few mornings to consider additional annual or temporary subscribers. Singer's son Cecil arrived from London. His nephew, Fred Singer, turned up from Paris. Sherwood Aldrich was in residence at White Villa. In the apartments, Vizcaya's architect F. Burrall Hoffman Jr. had checked in for an indefinite stay while designing Joseph Reiter's music room at Al Poniente, the former Cluett estate on North Lake Trail known as Bywater Lodge. Riter's palatial music room became home for the first events presented by the resort's Society of the Arts. Joining Hoffman was mural artist Robert Winthrop Chandler who was designing the murals for the music room, having also designed murals at Vizcaya.

On January 20, 1920, Mrs. F. Roosevelt Scovel hosted a luncheon at the Everglades Club to honor the new Mrs. Paris Singer, the former Joan Bates. In addition to being second cousin to President Theodore Roosevelt, Mrs. Scovel was also a granddaughter of President Ulysses S. Grant. To celebrate the club's first anniversary, a golf exhibition followed by a tea reception and dance were held February 4. William Robertson, the club's first golf professional, organized the event on the club's 2,830-yard course with a par of thirty-nine. The layout was modeled from famous links at Biarritz and Scotland. The one-hundred-fifty members and guests complained that the club was too small. Among the subscribers at the tea and dance celebrating the club's opening of the golf course were Mr. and Mrs. Richard Croker, Mr. J. Horace Harding, Sherwood Aldrich, Lord and Lady Queenborough, Mrs. Whitney Lyon, M. and Mrs. William Thaw, Mr. and Mrs. Leland Sterry, Michael P. Grace, and Dr. and Mrs. Landon Humphreys.

For the 1921 season, the club opened with Chef Jacques Lescarboura returning with "a galaxy of gourmet and epicure delights." Dr. Downs continued as club physician. Social columnists noted the club had developed a "welcome foreign atmosphere." Less than a week after the opening, the club had a waiting list of members and for accommodations.

By then, the club had grown beyond initial expectations. Singer was also involved in several real estate developments. What had been conceived as a relaxing escape and a refuge began to take a toll on Singer's health. In a June 14, 1922 letter to Mary and Bill Roberts in New York, Joan Singer invited the couple to Palm Beach the following winter and updated them on the latest comings-and-goings from Villa Les Rochers in St. Jean, Cap Ferrat. "Poor Paris has been quite ill with grippe and congestion of the lungs with a temperature of 104 for two or three days and an abnormally high blood pressure," Singer wrote. "He came downstairs yesterday for the first time in three weeks. It has made him awfully weak but with this lovely sunshine he will be getting strong again ..." In the midst of making sizable additions to the Everglades Club and new construction projects on Worth Avenue between 1923 and 1925, Paris Singer was involved with considerable developments in the North End.

In January 1923, the club opened without Singer's presence. At the opening gala, however, members and guests were joined by the sales force of Singer's Ocean and Lake Realty Company, the club's parent company.

Above. The first golf clubhouse was designed by architect Martin L. Hampton with a distinctive rooftop double-dome. *Historical Society of Palm Beach County.*

Below. The Everglades Club's 18-hole course was not completed until several years after the club first opened. *Historical Society of Palm Beach County*

While members were entertained, salesmen touted the latest available investments on Golf View Road, Singer Place, and the Blue Heron Inn resort proposed for the North End. Members also had their first glimpse of the new golf clubhouse designed by Martin L. Hampton, a former Mizner associate, and the completed eighteen-hole golf course.

For his Golf View Development Company, Singer retained New York architect Marion Sims Wyeth to build an ensemble of bijou houses, each of a different color on the road leading from the club to the ocean. Each house featured three master bedrooms and baths, servants' quarters, and a large living room. The Jay Carlisles were already in residence at Las Campanas. Across the street and situated on the golf course, E. F. and Marjorie Hutton occupied their stately cottage called Hogarcito. Across County Road and one block from the ocean extending from Gulfstream Road to Via Marina, Singer Place offered larger lots for home sites, where Wyeth designed his own residence Tre Fontane.

Within the clubhouse, the Great Hall's iron chandeliers were furnished with yellow parchment shades to make the light softer. Other recent additions included a Bridge Room located on the ground floor entered from the left side of the loggia. The Bridge Room was accessorized with colored theatrical gauze curtains detailed with green wool embroidery and up-to-date lighting. The newly added maisonettes that overlooked the tennis courts featured a wide second-floor loggia. The maisonettes' first seasonal residents were John Sanford, Alice DeLamar, Mrs. Lorenzo Woodhouse, Irenee du Pont, and Herbert M. Cowperthwaite. A seawall installed along the clubhouse's southwest perimeter allowed for a new filled-in area to make a large garden.

On Worth Avenue east of the clubhouse, the Everglades Arcade Shops opened with an array of boutiques: Jay Thorpe, Exotic Gardens, Miss Flora Darrah Silver, Palm Beach Decorative Society, furnishings from Wood, Edey & Slater and William Baumgarten, Max Littwitz lace shop, Ladd & Webb real estate, photographer Edward F. Foley's studio, gowns from Louis McCarthy, a hairdresser, a barber shop, and a Western Union office.

Following one of Palm Beach's most crowded seasons, where every train seat and hotel room was filled, Paris and Joan Singer retired to their villa in the south of France to recover. In a letter, Joan Singer described the work being done on their villa: "Paris has bought a lot more property and the scheme here is to be much bigger than Palm Beach! The new villa is unfinished but well on its way and we hope to be occupying it in October," she wrote. "We are getting furniture into the rooms that are furnished and Addison is expected here in July when we hope for great things. Paris is busy from morning to night and is well except for his high blood pressure for now as a result of his stupendous energy," Joan Singer concluded.

The activity both at the club and surrounding developments did not abate during the 1924 season as Singer continued to overload his health and work schedule. On March 8, *The New York Times* reported, "Paris Singer to retire; Give up control of Everglades Club." Because Singer was increasingly incapacitated by his health, he offered to sell the club to its four-hundred-twenty-five members. If each member agreed to pay $2,000, making for a purchase price of $850,000, members could purchase the club, the golf course, the tennis courts, maisonettes, and the villas. After several meetings, by the middle of March only half the membership had agreed to the purchase. Some members balked. Unable to reach an agreement by Singer's deadline, the offer to sell was withdrawn. Singer went ahead with plans for further development and expansion of the club.

In June 1925, Singer mortgaged the Everglades Club to buy an additional 5,200 feet of oceanfront to his North End holdings. With plans to house "thousands of pleasure-seekers" and deepening the inlet for sea-going yachts, Singer retained Addison Mizner to design the Blue Heron Beach Inn featuring a golf course and yacht harbor. Three months later, Singer announced plans to build a Venetian-style theater on the lakefront south of the Everglades Club where Flo Ziegfeld would stage his Follies during the winter. Pending its completion, Singer engaged Joseph Urban to redesign his Club Montmartre on Royal Palm Way to showcase Flo Ziegfeld's Palm Beach Follies. Ziegfeld promised that Palm Beach would host the first international beauty contest in search of a "Modern Cleopatra."

When the Everglades Club opened informally on December 15, 1925, members arrived as finishing touches were still being placed on the club's new façade and additions were being completed along Worth Avenue, including the iconic Via Mizner across the street. Two weeks later, when members celebrated New Year's Eve, the club's apartments, villas, and maisonettes were completely occupied. During the season, there was an avalanche of requests for membership. Maisonette leases were extended to W. Jackson Crispin, Cecil Singer, Princess Polignac, (aka Winaretta Singer, Paris Singer's sister); and George Singer. The cottages were occupied by Felix Doubleday, Leonard Schultze and Fullerton Weaver. While members were reluctant to buy the club from Singer, they hadn't lost any enthusiasm to support the club as its membership continued to grow.

During the previous summer, the clubhouse building entrance was completely rebuilt. On the second level, a row of apartments now extended east toward the arcade of shops. The new addition to the front of the club facing Worth Avenue would be reached by a circular staircase leading to the private apartments of Mr. and Mrs. Ralph Beaver Strassburger and Mr. and Mrs. James Donahue. Strassburger was president of the Singer Sewing Machine Company. On the south side, new apartments increased the club's seasonal capacity. The Harris Hammond apartment's loggia featured a domed Moorish roof and overlooked the golf course. A private party room with a sliding roof was added. Formerly the Court of Oranges, the Marble Patio's focal point was an oblong fountain with a goldfish pond lined with green tile and an octagonal tile top arising from the base with a symmetrical orange tree planted in the center. Tunisian tiles covered the entry space overlooking the patio. The ballroom/living room's rooftop was landscaped with shrubs, trees, vases, and jardinières. Reached from the apartment below

Above. The addition of the maisonettes added to the club's residential ambiance. *Library of Congress.*

by a flight of tiled steps, the roof garden was set aside for the exclusive use of Paris Singer whose apartment adjoined it.

A covered carriage entrance port cochere was attached to the east elevation together with a visitor's reception area. A new private ballroom or banqueting hall enhanced the east end of the east patio. Two nine-room cottages and three maisonettes were added. The club's villas were refurbished in the Spanish style. A new barber shop was built and two new garages added. New kitchens were installed and the dining room was redecorated with historic murals by Achille Angeli. The scenes depicted the Spanish Armada on the north wall. To the west, the smaller private dining room was adorned with frescoes of orange trees combined with Spanish crests, also designed by Angeli.

The Great Hall, the lounge and card rooms and the Orange Garden with terraced dancing floors, remain unchanged. To the south of the main club building, new gardens adjoined the golf links. Rising from the southwest corner of the gardens overlooking Singer Basin, a multi-story building housed English artist Oswald Birley's studio and the apartment.

Across from the clubhouse on Worth Avenue, a six-story office building on Via Parigi was completed. The first tenants were Grace Hyde's hat shop; La Tienda, Duchesse de Richelieu's antique import shop; Palm Beach Ocean Realty; H. C. Orrick, banker from Toledo; A. J. Drexel Biddle Jr.; and on the top floor, Singer's Ocean and Lake Realty. Via Parigi was comprised of twenty stores set on a winding pedestrian street that led to a courtyard plaza. Via Parigi's walls were tinted in cream, eau de Nile and blue. Among the tenants leasing second-floor apartments were architect Maurice Fatio and artist William Van Dresser.

Mortimer Singer, the son of Franklin Singer, was appointed the club's honorary secretary. Club policies remain unchanged, "... being more than ever like smart French and English clubs." Gala Nights would continue on Thursday and Sunday featuring the Meyer Davis orchestra. A House Committee was created to vet members' suggestions and complaints. The Board added Bylaw IV enabling "a few desirable young men, whose occupations prevent them from fully using the club, to become junior associate subscribers." The Club closed for the season on April 15.

Six miles to the north, Singer joined E. F. Hutton and other Everglades

Club members in building the Seminole Golf Club with an eighteen-hole course designed by Donald Ross. A golf pavilion was designed by Marion Sims Wyeth, containing dining rooms, sitting rooms, locker rooms, and a caddie house. The Everglades Club's harbor was dredged, cleaned and the bottom blasted to a six-foot depth. Along the oceanfront at Worth Avenue, Singer bought Gus's Bath, reserving a part of it as a private swim club for Everglades Club members.

Singer's enthusiasm for his Blue Heron development continued. He hired a thousand workers to complete his most speculative project. "My developments are purely the expansion of Palm Beach … I have been proceeding with the utmost caution …" Singer reassured investors. Despite Singer's public show of confidence, Florida's real estate pyramid was already showing signs of collapse. Mizner's Boca Raton was brought to a halt by a skittish market, construction embargoes and anxious investors.

And then, on April 9, 1927, Palm Beach awakened to the headline, "Florida authorities allege huge fraud. Singer bailed after arrest." While Paris Singer was exonerated of criminal fraud, numerous civil suits were filed by investors against him and his Palm Beach Ocean Realty Company. The North End developments were financed from mortgage bonds placed on the Everglades Club. These suits alleged Singer made off with more than $1.5 million under false pretenses. Singer lost these cases. Liens were filed against his Florida interests over the next several years.

For the 1930 season, Paris and Joan Singer did not stay at their Everglades Club apartment. Instead, they leased a cottage on Seaspray Avenue. In March, shortly after the club's annual Fancy Dress Ball, the Singers left Palm Beach never to return. With the club in a state of financial uncertainty, they encamped for a time on a houseboat on the Nile before heading to London. Several months after a Palm Beach County court lodged a $1.5 million lien against Singer, he died of heart failure in a London hotel room on June 23, 1932. Singer's obituary published in Great Britain never mentioned the thirteen years he spent in Palm Beach. He was entombed in the Singer vault at the family's Oldway estate in Paignton.

The aftermath

Singer's sons, Cecil and George Singer, represented the family's interest in dealings with the Everglades Club. Cecil succeeded his father as the

Above. While the Living Room is composed of many original furnishings as well as Mizner Industries tables and chairs, this immense room was first appointed with camelback sofas. *Library of Congress.*

Below. The Armada Dining Room's east wall once featured a balcony and an entrance from the Living Room with a wrought-iron gate. *Library of Congress.*

club's president until the 1933 season. In August 1933, Cecil and the bond holders placed the Everglades Club Company's real estate in receivership, appointing local real estate agent John L. Webb as their receiver. Cecil Singer and his brother, Paris Graham Singer, representing the family's Canadian-based syndicates holding the stock and notes of the club's parent company, filed a lawsuit alleging the Everglades Club owed them more than $200,000. The suit claimed officers and directors of the club fraudulently appropriated money. They also filed a damage suit to recover $375,000 in promissory notes, recorded in March 1928.

After the Singer family filed their lawsuit against the club, the club's members, led by Hugh Dillman and John Shephard, filed for involuntary bankruptcy of the club itself apart from the real estate. Columnist Cholly Knickerbocker reported an "explosion in the Everglades Club, as far as management policy." At the time, the club's directors explored several options for the club to continue operation in a post-Singer era. In January 1934, James Cromwell advocated opening the club to the public between the hours of ten p.m. and two a.m. each day except Thursday and Sunday. A favorable nine-to-one vote was recorded. It was decided to ask the receiver

Above. The 1925 additions included an arcade leading east from the Great Hall to the port cochere entrance. *Library of Congress*.

to petition the court for such authority. Several weeks later, Charlton Yarnall reported the court would not approve the open night policy because it affected the club's exclusivity and might thwart the solicitation of new members.

Charles Munn suggested members be permitted to issue invitational cards permitting guests to use the Orange Gardens during prescribed times. Yarnall proposed a Committee of Ladies be formed for the purpose of sponsoring teas in the Orange Gardens on Saturday afternoons. Both the Munn plan and Yarnall's suggestions were approved. At one point, club members considered selling the club to the Town of Palm Beach, opening it to residents as a public golf course. Following a tour of the club's facilities by the mayor and council, public officials balked at the cost that could only be approved with a referendum.

After several years of acrimonious wrangling, the club's future was finally settled in January 1936 when a group of club members formed The Everglades Protective Syndicate. The syndicate bought the club and its real estate holdings for the existing debt and $450,000 from the trusteeship held by the Central Farmers Trust and H. C. Rorick. A decade later, the Everglades Club became member-owned when each of its eight hundred members paid a thousand dollars to become an equal shareholder of the club and its holdings.

Described at the time of his death as "one of the most picturesque and important figures in the history of Palm Beach," Singer was consumed by Florida's Land Boom during the 1920s where he amassed and lost a fortune. As a result, Paris Singer's noteworthy legacy was eclipsed by his unsuccessful development ventures where he destabilized the Everglades Club's financial future by pledging the club's holdings as collateral. Ultimately, Singer may have been the man who " ... made Palm Beach beautiful," introduced the work of architect Addison Mizner, built the Everglades Club, and transformed Worth Avenue into a world-class address but his imprudent real estate dealings relegated him to the town's rogue's gallery rather than its pantheon of leaders. Although his memory continues to be overshadowed by his financial transgressions, Paris Singer was the man whose imagination and vision transformed Palm Beach from a seasonal resort town into a cosmopolitan international destination.

Above. The expansive loggia at Casa Florencia was among Palm Beach's architectural treasures. *Historical Society of Palm Beach County.*

8

CASA FLORENCIA

A GREATER GRANDEUR

How one of the town's extraordinary mansions could be admired and appreciated in 1923 and three decades later be considered useless in 1950 when it was demolished makes for one of Palm Beach's fascinating rise-and-fall chronicles. Reminiscent of the priceless artifacts unearthed from archeological excavations documenting ancient civilizations, an architectural dig at a South End oceanfront vacant lot would most likely uncover the ruins of one of Addison Mizner's architectural masterpieces. Contemporaneous newspaper accounts on Casa Florencia's demise reported that the grass-covered elevated mound at 910 South Ocean Boulevard entombs the ocean-to-lake estate's structural elements, possibly including Gothic windows, Italian statuary, Salamanca paneling, Renaissance doors, Florentine marble railings, and a bas-relief bust of Addison Mizner.

Casa Florencia's owners, Florence Brokaw Martin Satterwhite, and her husband, Dr. Preston Pope Satterwhite, were regarded among the era's most prominent collectors of sixteenth- and seventeenth-century Spanish and Italian furnishings and art works. Mizner and Florence Satterwhite were friends from the architect's New York days when she was known as Widow Martin. In 1906, she traveled with Mizner on his first known visit to Palm Beach. So however savvy and demanding the couple proved as clients, especially during 1923 when there were twelve other considerable projects on the drawing tables at the architect's studio, Mizner and the Satterwhites succeeded in creating a magnificent house.

The de Medicis of South Ocean Boulevard

The 1880s marriage of Florence Brokaw to Standard Oil executive James E. Martin had joined two of New York's prominent families. The daughter of William Vail Brokaw, a prosperous merchant, Florence led a gilded life between her 803 Fifth Avenue apartment and Martin Hall, the couple's posh Long Island estate. Her privileged life was shattered in 1905 when her husband was killed in a Christmas Eve car accident. Her grief was eased when she became the principal beneficiary of husband James Martin's $15 million fortune. It was during this period she and Addison Mizner developed a friendship. At the time, Mizner also lived on Long Island and kept an office on Park Avenue.

But the popular heiress was again struck by tragedy when her son contracted typhoid fever in Rome and died in Paris. It was then, according to some stories, she met Dr. Preston Pope Satterwhite, a New York surgeon, who was called in to treat her son. According to other accounts, Florence and Dr. Satterwhite first met during an evening at the Metropolitan Opera.

Whatever the couple's first encounter, their July 1908 marriage at Florence's Long Island estate was followed by a three-month honeymoon. Soon after, Dr. Satterwhite packed away his scalpel and scrubs to devote full-time to his more aesthetic interests, art collecting and entertaining. The newlyweds called in the Olmsted Brothers firm to spruce up Martin Hall's landscape into a more baronial setting. Their shared passion for Spanish and Italian Renaissance art works and artifacts made them as familiar figures in Tuscan churchyards as Parke-Bernet's auction galleries.

The great mansions of 1923

By the time the Satterwhites were ready to join Palm Beach's cottage colony, Paris Singer and Addison Mizner had already turned Palm Beach's rambling oceanfront cottages into a more noticeable Mediterranean port-of-call. Some of the earlier less imposing villas were enlarged with grand entrance halls and dining rooms rescaled for banquet-sized repasts. With the ongoing real estate boom escalating, Palm Beachers were aspiring to a greater grandeur, according to architectural historian Donald W. Curl in his book, *Mizner's Florida*.

For the Satterwhites, Mizner designed what Curl described as, "...

Above. The Mizner designed staircase was lost when the Casa Florencia was demolished.
Historical Society of Palm Beach County.

a larger and more elegant version of the Villa Flora," the North Ocean Boulevard mansion designed for Edward Shearson. Casa Florencia's first-floor plan followed Villa Flora's, with a formal entrance and central staircase facing north on Clarendon Avenue. To the right of the formal gallery hall, a two-story guest wing ran parallel to Clarendon; to the left, the library, dining room, and living room were sited sequentially along South Ocean Boulevard. The dining room was connected to the main house by a cloister much like the Warden House, another of Mizner's celebrated 1923 commissions. According to Curl, however effusive the Satterwhites' guests were about the "cathedral-like atmosphere and intricate carvings that made the room a place of beauty," they found the Gothic chapel ambience "not an altogether cheerful place to dine."

Following their medieval feast, guests often retreated to the loggia and garden for the evening's entertainment. The loggia's arched ceiling

Above. Furnished with authentic Renaissance artworks and furnishings from Addison Mizner's Bunker Road factory, the Satterwhites' living room was traced from the architect's floor plan for Villa Flora, the Edward Shearson villa on North Ocean Boulevard. *Historical Society of Palm Beach County.*

was painted Mizner green, said to be the first place this distinctive tint, synonymous with Palm Beach, was ever applied. Above the loggia, a stylish roof garden was lined with Italian statuary. When not entertaining the Duchesse de Richelieu or local royalty, such as Eva and Ned Stotesbury, the Renaissance devotees hosted musicales for several hundred guests on their moonlit patio. Metropolitan Opera soprano Frances Alda performed selections from Gounod's opera, *Romeo and Juliet*, from one of the bedroom balconies. On the terrace, vocalists brought in from New York staged the second act of *Madame Butterfly*. Following the evening's program, there was dancing to a full orchestra in the garden before guests enjoyed an after-midnight buffet.

To show their appreciation for Mizner's endeavor, the Satterwhites had sculptor Percival Dietsch craft a bas relief likeness of the architect to adorn a window keystone. Featured in a 1926 issue of *Arts and Architecture* magazine, Casa Florencia was among Mizner's most theatrical settings.

Given to wearing a diamond tiara, Florence Satterwhite's particular flair caught the attention of *The New York Times* when a March 1926 story was headlined, "Palm Beach stirred by social rivalry: Mrs. Satterwhite is considered latest aspirant to leadership of colony." Whatever her social rank, it was short lived. In May 1927, she died following a brief illness at the Plaza Hotel, leaving Dr. Satterwhite a widower with a considerable fortune.

Vowing to never again occupy the villa, Dr. Satterwhite headed to Egypt, placing Casa Florencia on the market. He bought Martin Hall from her estate, rechristening it Preston Hall. Later, he acquired a two-story apartment for $450,000 at 960 Fifth Avenue, the highest price ever paid for a New York apartment at the time.

From palace to pit

Two years later, Casa Florencia was sold to John North Willys, an automobile manufacturer from Toledo, Ohio. Before World War I, the Willys-Overland Company was the nation's second largest auto producer; only Ford Motor Company was more productive. By the early 1930s, the market collapsed and the company was bankrupt. Despite the downturn, Willys had secured a substantial personal fortune. A Republican stalwart, Willys was appointed the first American ambassador to Poland.

Willys and his wife Isabel spent only a few seasons in Palm Beach before the couple divorced in 1934. John Willys quickly remarried. However, only a few months after taking a new bride, Willys died from a heart attack while attending the Kentucky Derby. The court fight over Willys' fortune and Casa Florencia between the second Mrs. Willys and her stepdaughter Virginia Willys Aguirre made headlines, with Willys' daughter eventually winning the Mizner house.

During World War II, many Palm Beach houses remained shuttered with some not reopening until the mid-1950s. Assembly-line products and subdivisions flourished as Americans equated luxury with vacuum cleaners and kitchen appliances rather than Old World craftsmanship. The Hurricane of 1947 was as devastating as the infamous 1928 storm, especially to the oceanfront in the South End.

In 1949, Virginia Willys de Landa, now married to Jose de Landa – who reportedly hailed from "an old Argentinian family" – retained architect Howard Chilton to design a one-story ranch house with jalousie windows that would replace Casa Florencia. "Home too large, Owner declares," read newspaper headlines, as Virginia de Landa said she was "tired of living in a museum and wants to live in something more modern and comfortable." Plans went forward to raze Casa Florencia, believed to be the first of Mizner's great Palm Beach houses to be demolished. Routinely, the fragmentary remains of Palm Beach houses were carted away in a truck.

Oddly, Virginia de Landa arranged to have a bunker-like pit excavated on her property between where her new house would be built facing Clarendon and South Ocean Boulevard. A twenty-six foot deep crater was dug extending two-hundred feet along South Ocean Boulevard and one-hundred feet on Clarendon Avenue. It took sixty-five workmen, several bulldozers, and one crane to pulverize Casa Florencia. One month later, Addison Mizner's magnificent sandcastle, once a measure of Palm Beach's greater grandeur, was gone.

No sooner had the de Landas moved into their new ranch house, now fortified from the ocean by a noticeable bunker, when the couple divorced. Virginia married and divorced again, before she hitched up with Wilson Charles Lucom, a well-known "anti-Communist Democrat" from Washington, D.C. It was Lucom who put 910 South Ocean Boulevard back

Above. The dining room's Romanesque ambience gave the Satterwhites' guests the sense of being in a medieval monastery. *Historical Society of Palm Beach County.*

*Above.*To show their appreciation of Addison Mizner's work, Florence and Preston Satterwhite adorned a window keystone with a bas-relief likeness of the architect. *Historical Society of Palm Beach County.*

Below. Casa Florencia was demolished more than fifty years ago; its architectural fragments buried along the site's eastern frontage along Ocean Boulevard. In 2015, the property's owners unearthed the buried architectural fragments. *Photography Augustus Mayhew.*

in the headlines.

Following his wife's death, the six-acre ocean-to-lake estate, now platted as the Lucom Subdivision, was sold during the early 1990s for more than $14 million to a rumored Saudi prince. Although Ocean Bay Holdings LTD, a Bahamas-based company said to represent the Mideast royal, received approvals for a more than 50,000-square-foot estate, some ARCOM members complained the house looked "more Miami than Mizner." Nevertheless, the massive mansion was never built on the oceanfront lot, although Ocean Bay sold the vacant lots along Clarendon Avenue. Two decades later, the South Ocean Boulevard lot remains vacant.

Above. Judge James R. Knott kept a detailed diary of the marriages he officiated for many prominent Palm Beach brides and grooms and the backyard and ballroom receptions that followed. *Historical Society of Palm Beach County.*

9

TYING THE KNOT
A PALM BEACH WEDDING DIARY

Dear friends: You are entering into the holy estate which is the deepest mystery of experience and the very sacrament of divine love ... You are performing an act of utter faith, believing in each other to the utmost, Amid the seeming reality of present imperfection believe in the ideal. The *Honorable James R. Knott.*

Palm Beach weddings have never attracted the same spotlight as the town's divorces, their breathless headlines detailed by vigilant court stenographers. As the years go on, that first white-dress-walk-down–the-aisle moment may be but a hazy memory, considering there might have been a number of other bouquets, cake cuttings and exchange of vows. From the onset, marriage was as respected a sport at Palm Beach as tennis or golf.

A noted historian and local circuit judge, The Honorable James R. Knott's diary recorded his impressions of the many weddings he performed on Palm Beach from 1968 to 1993. Here are excerpts from Judge Knott's diary on many a Palm Beach "to have and to hold from this day forward ...."

October 19, 1968

Alfred William Lasher Jr. to Jeanne Helene See Perry

239 Emerald Lane, the bride's home

After the ceremony, the party was attended by the Alfonso Fanjuls, Ambassador Stanton Griffis, Paul Rogers, Chris Dunphy, Loy and Therese Anderson, and Helen and Bill Cluett. The bride became ill but came down after dinner was served. The toast: "To Jeanne, Who I wean is indeed a glamour queen, one of the most beautiful too. It is not to you alone we drink, But to your future, we tink."

February 2, 1969

John Kress Williams to Sandra Julia Rousseau

250 Kawama Lane

The ceremony was followed by a reception, which was large indeed. A tent covered the backyard with carpets over the grass and tables were filled with flowers. There were two bars at each end of the tent, a large buffet, Cliff Hall's orchestra of ten or more, and a dance floor, which got as crowded as a nightclub. Everybody was there, old and young, American and Cuban, blending happily. Many Palm Beach notables of all ages, as well as Ft. Lauderdale and Miami, an attractive mixture, including Mrs. Bernard Gimbel, the Fanjuls, Albert Bostwick and his wife Mollie Netcher Bostwick, and Nicky and Bunny du Pont were there. My first visit with them in a long time.

The groom (twice-divorced) led his bride out on the dance floor for the first dance with a neat small-step waltz. Only the family attended the wedding. The bride's father, who came out of Cuba at Castro's assumption of power, is a slender, ascetic looking man. (Note: The Aspuru sisters were once called the "Cuban Cushing sisters.") Lourdes Aspuru is an intelligent, perceptive woman, with a delicacy of feeling and warmth. Although living in Madrid the past three years, she immediately called by name all the many people who came by her and chatted about their affairs with perfect familiarity.

May 11, 1970

Ignacio Llanos to Lourdes Aspuru

270 Kawama Lane

Dr. Llanos is a lawyer, residing in Madrid but a native of Barcelona. The bride was the former Mrs. Musso, then Mrs. George Rich (nephew of Elmer Rich). She is a native of Havana and has lately been in Madrid. They will live in Madrid where they have a discotheque. At the ceremony there was only the family, but what a family, many, many sisters or sisters-in-law, three brothers-in-law, the bride's parents, several children, plus a few scattered relatives, Loy and Therese Anderson, Mollie Netcher Bostwick with a new friend named Paul Wilmot, and Charles Amory, who is a companion of the bride's sister, Julia Rousseau.

The groom was highly imperfect in repeating certain required words back during the ceremony. They had been written out for him by Pepito, a relative, so that he could read them in giving his response. This very nearly led to the collapse of the ceremony. He continued reading past the place and into the next response before I asked him. All this led to giggles by the young girl serving as ring bearer, echoed by her friends in the rear. At several points I thought I would break into uncontrollable laughter but the tension of the occasion carried us through.

Lourdes now marries a young man, who is tall, dark, and mostly handsome, among whose most notable qualities is a kind of boyishness. A supper of Spanish food followed, some of which [was] cooked by the Aspuru family and brought from Madrid. These Cuban-Spanish people are impressive in their sense of self-composure. Sometimes giving the impression of being impassive; yet, they do yield after a thawing-out period. Strong family people, not at the ready with strangers. The Fanjuls are very outgoing, a strong exception.

May 25, 1970

Keith Sutton to Lena "Bobbie" Vogel

Sanford Avenue

He is a lawyer, formerly of New York/Los Angeles, 50, now making his headquarters in Palm Beach as head of a Book-of-the-Month Club. She is the widow of the president of Metro-Goldwyn-Mayer (Joe Vogel just died last year, written up in Louis Nizer's book), 55, a rather fragile, delicate, sensitive appearing creature, emotional, slightly passive. Her son, Richard Vogel, just of Tulane Law School, was there with his young wife. He, in the Marines; Bobbie's daughter, 21, also there. All attractive. About 15-18 people, or more. Champagne.

February 12, 1971

Arnold Winfield "Chip" Chapin to Laura Chastain

Laura Chastain, 56, divorced wife of Sam Chastain and mother of Tom Chastain, an eligible bachelor, married in a ceremony in my hearing chamber with a Navy Chief and the bride's son Tom present. The groom's father was VP of General Motors. His mother, as an old lady of 83, allowed herself to become involved with a fortune hunting local "physician," a married man with four children who pretended to be infatuated with her. Mrs. Chastain and Sam were divorced more than fifteen years ago. He was a Georgia cracker, and clever enough to amass several million in land and cattle, cared more for his Wyoming ranch than Palm Beach. He was a member of the Cluett family with old Palm Beach ties. They became disenchanted with their marriage and separated before divorcing, preceding his death in middle age.

A few friends, a little dancing and a big wedding cake can make for one of the most beautiful days in anyone's life.

Above. Judge Knott's Wedding Diary. *Historical Society of Palm Beach County*

July 26, 1972

Dr. James B. Craig Jr. to Jane Wheeler Irby Lihme Obolensky von Ruekfrang

A fourth marriage for each. The ceremony was performed at my office with three or four friends present and a professional photographer. The bride is a baroness by her last marriage to Palm Beacher John Anthony Ruecker. He had changed his birth name to what he claimed was his "birthright" name, Johan Antonio Baron von Ruekfrang. Jane was formerly known as Princess Obolensky, when married to Obie, who was for years her husband.

She is in real estate and is known as a bridge and backgammon player. He is a prominent man, a rather hefty fellow and likable. He seemed to have various moods during the ceremony. He made sounds and would then lower his head to rest on his bride's shoulder during the short ceremony. They invited me to dinner at The Beach Club. And when I told them I had to go home for my houseguests, they invited my houseguests, too. I later heard that by the time the wedding party arrived at The Breakers, they were beyond the eating stage.

28 July 1972

Charles Minot Amory to Julia Rousseau

The Loy Anderson house

Only the Andersons (Loy and Therese), Sandra Rousseau Williams (married by me in 1969), her younger sister and her husband, and Minot Amory, Charles' son (now living in Gulf Stream) were present. Huge flower displays (courtesy of The Flower Cart shop, owned by the groom) through the entire first floor of the house. I did not accept an invitation to join a larger group at Julia's after the ceremony. Charles Amory's bride is the former wife of Enrique Rousseau, the present husband of Lilly Pulitzer, who was the former wife of Charles' half-brother Peter Pulitzer.

August 25, 1972

Cesare Zavaglia to Victoria Bertha Schrafft

315 Tangier Avenue

Brownie McLean, presently the wife of Jock McLean, is the mother of the bride, as she is the former Mrs. George Schrafft. She was there, of course, with Mary Sanford and a good many socialites (a word I do not care for). Jock's former wife is married to Jimmy Stewart, the movie actor; his brother Ned is married to the former Mrs. Alfred Vanderbilt, Wendy's mother. Ivy Baker Priest and the county sheriff were also there. The Schrafft house is not large, although it is an unusually beautiful setting. The guests, who were served a buffet with champagne, just about overran the place.

March 5, 1974

James Anthony "Tony" Boalt to Maria "Toinette" Rousseau Cochran

250 Kawama Lane

A second marriage for both. A huge tent took up the entire backyard. A full orchestra played. Flowers were in great profusion. The bride's father, Enrique Rousseau and his bride, Lilly, were there. Everyone was there and it was a social bust.

June 15, 1974

Claude Cartier to Sandra Julia Williams, nee Rousseau

She is a native of Cuba; he is native of Hungary and of the Cartier jewelry family. His first marriage ended in the divorce; hers in the death of her husband Jake Williams in 1971, only two years after I married them in the same house as the present wedding. Only the family and a few guests including Stan Rumbaugh and his attractive wife. The Cartiers will live at his apartment at One Beekman Place.

July 12, 1976

Charles Faegre to Patricia Blake Hilton

695 South County Road

His first; her second. She is the widow of Nicky Hilton, (he died in 1969) once married to Elizabeth Taylor. Trish is a native of Alabama. Trish Hilton is a dark-haired beauty, slender, medium height, natural and unaffected, much like her mother (Pat Schmidlapp). He looks 39 to 45; she looks to be in her 20s. The groom, a Washington lawyer. He is a good fellow, genial. The groom's mother was unpretentious and well-mannered.

About 16 to 18 for the ceremony, held in a Florida room with bowers of flowers. There was a best man but no bridesmaids. The bride's stepfather, Horace Schmidlapp, gave her away. Guests arrived en masse at 6:30 p.m. Mary Sanford, Loy Anderson Jr. with his new Swedish bride, a tall, willowy type with well-molded features. Also attending were Mary and Philip Hulitar and Jimmy and Dottie dePeyster. People, I understand, from New York, DC, Los Angeles, and Minneapolis. Good-looking (or as much as nature and artifice could allow) well-mannered. Hordes of servants bearing goodies, champagne. I left after about thirty minutes of this.

January 11, 1982

John C. Noble to Cristina Fernanda de Heeren

Louwana, 473 North County Road

I left before the ceremony was finalized by a Catholic priest (with robe) who blessed the rings. Among those present, Mr. and Mrs. Douglas Fairbanks Jr., Virginia Munn, Mrs. Fernanda ("Nonie") Munn Kellogg, Bunny DuPont, Mrs. Alfonso Fanjul, and Edgar Mitchell, the astronaut. An unbelievably beautiful scene with flowers everywhere. The bride's father, Rodman A. deHeeren, who was not well, came down an elevator and escorted his daughter to two kneeling blocks, preceded by two small children, carrying flowers.

The guests were asked to hum "Here Comes the Bride." The ceremony was followed by a gathering of friends in a heated tent.

April 18, 1987

Ralph Levitz to Mary Jacqueline Broadway Smith

1520 South Ocean Boulevard

He is a native of Pennsylvania; she of Louisiana, Southern accent retained. His sixth; her third. The house is just south of the Wideners' place, ocean to lake, a pretty enough spread but not a showplace. The house is Spanish.

Tables were set for ten, about three tables on the patio, and more tables on the terrace overlooking the pool. Many chairs were brought in for the guests, about 90. Ralph Levitz, a small man, neat and compact not as chatty, has a preoccupied air. He said he is a stock trader and keeps his eye on the ticker all day. He had six groomsmen. He and I, and they, entered the pool area from the north; the bride (with six bridesmaids) from the steps, to meet in a little arbor for the ceremony. Then cocktails served by at least 15 waiters, male and female, flying around. The bride, accompanied by a man named Archie. The guests were all seated. Finally, dinner. Undoubtedly expensive, five or six courses, which roughly took two hours. I left after the entree as it was already ten o'clock.

The bride was blonde, rather pretty and chatty. She had redecorated the house (glassy chrome and modern stuff). She appeared overstimulated contrary to the groom. She had come to my office three days before the ceremony with a $500 check for the Historical Society. She has been in Palm Beach less than a year and doubtless, hopes for a future unclouded by economic concerns. She has been selling real estate.

NOTE: After Ralph Levitz died in 1995, Mrs. Levitz left Palm Beach for Vicksburg. Several months later, she went missing, leaving only a blood trail. Her body was never been found.

September 23, 1987

Joseph Jordan Eller, MD, 91(!), to Lucille Marguerite (Pillow) Vaughan, 79

Marriage performed at her hospital room (emphysema) in St. Mary's Hospital with "Chuck" Wilson Lucom (former husband of Virginia Willys de Aguirre de Landa, who died), and one, Harry Lee Elkins, present — and also a young couple related to Elkins. The bride, who comes from

Canada, is very outgoing, hearty, and intelligent. I have known Dr. Eller, Palm Beach's "doctor diplomat," who had JFK as a patient and is still in practice, and appears to be only about 75, and has treated me a couple of times. He is a former polo player with the likes of King Alfonso, who was married to the daughter of the president of Mexico, or some such. He likes to tell of his famous friends and companions in days gone by. I think the new wife may be very well off. He spoke of her children's strong objection to the marriage. But and however, I believe him to be well meaning and not too designing, maybe it's true love.

October 17, 1987

Peter Leland Amory to Lisa Belle Parbus Kotter (nee Fields)

250 Kawama Lane, home of Charles Amory, the groom's father

Charles Amory's sister, Grace Amory, once famous in golf, was there, charming as ever, but his cousin Nonie (Fernanda Munn Kellogg) was in the hospital and his aunt, Dorothy Spreckels Munn was in the hospital. Lilly Pulitzer and her present husband, Enrique Rousseau (former husband of Mrs. Amory, the hostess) were there. There were about 35 guests. Champagne and cocktails were served on trays. Four tables of eight to ten people for a well-served dinner, with Charles Amory presiding afterward. He's now 71. He told me I had previously married seven couples in his house. I also saw four other couples that I had married. I sat to the right of the hostess. She is a pretty woman, her complexion a combination of soft shades, essentially very light and soft pink. I gave a toast to the bride, "beautiful and radiant." Many others followed.

November 25, 1989

Robert Thomas Eigelberger to Susan Grace Cochran Phipps

Grace Trail

She is the daughter of Mike and Molly Phipps. The bride and groom had a strong tendency to giggle and laugh during the ceremony in which they were joined by their friends. It was held outside, in perfect weather, by a fountain in a large courtyard at his place on Grace Trail. Just afterward, I left for her place, too soon, because a cocktail party ensued.

Her place is seemingly isolated in the woods with a large open space, several acres, bordered on all sides by these woods. The site was almost unbelievable, like a movie set up. On the grass was a large tent, alive and blazing with multi-colored lights with dozens of tables. The music was good. Outside, the guests were having just one more wandered at will or stood in clumps. I found Clippie (Mrs. Ben Phipps) of Tallahassee and she asked me to eat with her, which I did. The bride was perfect, pretty and poised; Bob, the groom, was all energy.

Above. Judge Knott's Wedding Diary. *Historical Society of Palm Beach County*

Above. In 1982 Judge Knott married John Noble and Cristina de Heeren, pictured above in a portrait with her mother Aimée de Heeren, at Louwana, the de Heeren's home and one of Palm Beach's most romantic settings. *Augustus Mayhew Photography.*

Above. The Palm Beach Story, movie poster. *Library of Congress.*

10

PALM BEACH UNCOUPLED

In 1959 lovelorn expert and lifelong Palm Beacher Barbara Hutton famously told the press after she sacked her sixth husband: "Marriage? Divorce? What are they but scraps of paper? I am in no hurry to go through that crazy routine again."

Nevertheless, the former deb -- once a countess and a baroness as well as thrice a princess -- became seven times a divorcee, following her final *au revoir* to Laotian Prince Pierre Raymond Doan. Her tally of marital dissolutions exceeded by three those of her aunt, Palm Beach grand dame Marjorie Merriweather Post Close Hutton Davies May, who made it simpler on everybody by reverting to her maiden name after her last divorce in 1964.

Palm Beach's divorce game has never grown old, played with the same skill once required at the dice table or roulette wheel inside Bradley's Beach Club. Most any seasoned Palm Beacher knows how Henry M. Flagler legally parted with his second wife, the institutionalized Alice, after state lawmakers favored him in 1901 by making it legal to divorce on grounds of insanity. Ever since Flagler scrapped the "in sickness and in health, and forsaking all others, until death do us part" from his marriage vows, any number of marital shipwrecks have been driven by the belief that anyone could get a divorce in Florida without delay or trouble.

In sharp contrast to the stigma that divorce inflicted on women of less wealth and eminence on the mainland, Palm Beach break-ups have been so pervasive that some assume it a prerequisite for residency. The divorced Duchess of Windsor's notoriety, for instance, only made her more appealing to the island's denizens. Margaret Emerson McKim Vanderbilt Baker Amory's ever-lengthening calling card never jeopardized their social standing. And who was surprised that the plot of the iconic madcap comedy film *The Palm Beach Story* involved Claudette Colbert's character heading for Palm Beach to get a divorce and marry a rich man?

No balm for Countess Salm

For his 1925 song "Poor Little Rich Girl," Noel Coward penned: *"In lives of leisure, the craze for pleasure steadily grows; Cocktails and laughter, but what comes after? Nobody knows!"* Coward might well have been writing about Standard Oil heiress Millicent Rogers, styled Countess Salm, when she shed her first husband, Count Ludwig von Salm-Hoogstraeten, in 1927. Countess Salm fled Europe and sought refuge with her son Peter at Palm Beach, turning the town into a daily international dateline. Dueling telegrams shrieked charges and countercharges of abandonment, desertion and kidnapping.

When Count Ludwig arrived at Palm Beach accompanied by his patrons, who happened to be a tabloid editor and publisher, the awaiting crowds clamored for photographs and autographs. In between tennis matches, the apparent no-account count was approached to model for fashion magazines and promote local real estate offices.

In response, Countess Salm armed her servants with handguns, hiring detectives for round-the-clock protection. Eventually, the count returned without his son but reportedly with $300,000 from his father-in-law. Several months later, Countess Salm was granted a Paris divorce. Discarding her tiara and title, she married Argentine Arturo Peralta Ramos. That marriage – and a third – also didn't last.

On what grounds?

A *New York Times* headline in February 1927 read, "Divorce Boom at Palm Beach." While Nevada's Reno reigned as the nation's quickie-divorce destination, primarily due to its six-week residency requirement, it meant

Above. Margaret Emerson McKim Vanderbilt Baker Amory. After her divorce from Charles Amory, Margaret Emerson reclaimed her maiden name. *Library of Congress*

Above. Consuelo Vanderbilt, Duchess of Marlborough. After separating from the Duke of Marlborough in 1906, Consuelo Vanderbilt's marriage was not annulled until 1925 when she became free to marry French aviator Jacques Balsan. *Library of Congress*

the wealthy had to endure campfires and horseback rides while they awaited their turns to be "Reno-vated," as society wags put it. Not wanting to lose its attraction as a laissez-faire mecca, Florida loosened its divorce standards. Unlike New York, Florida permitted a variety of grounds for dissolving a match, making Palm Beach's county courthouse the last chapter for many of the resort's hopeless twosomes.

In 1930, when Florence Crozer split from John Rutherfurd, she accused him of torture. Margaret Amory won her 1934 case against Charles Amory, claiming he suffered from habitual intemperance. In 1945, three days after Ailsa Mellon Bruce -- regarded then as the wealthiest woman in the world -- threw out husband David Bruce, charging mental cruelty and desertion, he was honeymooning in Virginia with the new Mrs. Bruce, Evangeline Bell. New York lawyer Dudley Field Malone even established Palm Beach and Paris offices, allowing clients to file for a Parisian divorce while on their Florida holiday. "Divorcing by way of Paris has become a recognized industry at Palm Beach," noted *The Times*.

After Royal Palm Way residents Reggie and Phyllis Brooks' case played out at the county courthouse in the summer of 1930, newspaper reports stated "moving picture personages from Hollywood," in discussing the case, "were of the opinion that if the Palm Beach couple were to re-enact madcap highlights of their one-year married life for the screen, they could make more than $1 million." Mrs. Brooks complained she had suffered a nervous breakdown after her husband filled their marital bed with bread crumbs and sliced grapefruits. He was said to have greeted her guests dressed as a clown with a green hat and run screaming into her bedroom as well as ringing cowbells and slamming doors at all hours and wearing only a nightshirt for three days. As it turned out, she settled for the $200,000 Palm Beach house rather than a Hollywood close-up.

Breaking up badly

John and Josephine Cooper's Palm Beach romance may have only lasted a month, but their 1930s divorce proceedings lasted a year. In court documents, Josephine alleged she was dragged to Cooper's Ocean Boulevard mansion and told to either give him $100,000 or he would take her life. She told the court she escaped to Miami. When her husband found her, he demanded $7,500 and a new automobile, which she agreed to provide if he released her, according to testimony. Unbound, she fled to the police.

The split between Russell A. Firestone Jr, and his third wife, Mary Alice, aroused even the most subdued. Their two-year court battle in the mid-1960s was fueled by accusations of adultery, cruelty and more -- with a hundreds witnesses called. According to court documents, The Honorable Judge James R. Knott at one point remarked during the proceedings that the case was "enough to make Dr. Freud's hair curl," with Mr. Firestone displaying "the erotic zest of a satyr." In any event, the Firestone divorce was finally granted in 1967 on grounds of mental cruelty.

As compelling as the Firestone case became, its shock and awe diminished after Peter and Roxanne Pulitzer made megaton headlines when they squared off during the 1980s in a case that was nothing if not titillating. And after all was said and done, Roxanne Pulitzer was deprived of a substantial settlement from Peter Pulitzer. The 18-month ordeal was turned into a television movie and embroiled friends of the Pulitzers, Jim and Jacqui Kimberly. When the Kimberlys' divorced four years later, they also grabbed headlines.

In the meantime, Roxanne became a divorce-case regular, going from respondent to appellant to witness to petitioner within a few court calendars. Although during her trial Roxanne denied anything more than a business relationship with Count Jean de la Moussaye, she was called to testify when the count and his wife, Francine, split in 1991. Later, Roxanne's subsequent forty-nine-day marriage to John Haggin Jr. brought her a six-figure settlement.

And long before he was a presidential candidate married to third wife Melania, Donald Trump was nearly as well-known in Palm Beach for his splits with Ivana (in 1991) and the former Marla Maples (in 1999). Czech-born Ivana even wrote a how-to book: *The Best is Yet to Come: Coping with Divorce and Enjoying Life Again*. Her take on marital endings reflected her well-known wit: "Don't get mad," she said. "Get everything!"

What price goodbye?

These days, Palm Beachers do seem more interested in knowing "How much?" than wincing at the outrageous and the wicked. In 1994, Claudia Cohen's staggering $80 million package from deal-maker Ron Perelman set tongues wagging. A decade later, Laura and Greg Norman called it quits after a twenty-six-year marriage, with Mrs. Norman banking more than $100 million, according to published reports.

And while we may never know the dollar amount of billionaire Ken Griffin's recent out-of-court agreement with his wife, Anne, the seven year

Above. Marjorie Merriweather Post Close Hutton Davies May. *Library of Congress.*

battle between Elena and Russian fertilizer mogul Dmitry Rybolovlev --
termed the most expensive in the world, ever -- was resolved in October
2015 by a Swiss court. Among the disputed evidence presented was the
Rybolovlev seaside estate at 515 N. County Road, which Trump had sold
for $95 million – a record price -- in 2008. Although a Swiss judge reduced
Elena's $4.8 billion payout to $604 million, the couple settled for an
undisclosed amount -- close to $1 billion, according to some reports, when
she threatened an appeal to the Swiss Supreme Court.

All of which leads us to a statement as true for Flagler-era millionaires
as today's hedge-fund billionaires: In Palm Beach, when matrimony leads
to testimony, when forevermore becomes nevermore, the stakes can be
high indeed.

Above. Although King Edward VIII's abdication and marriage to Wallis Simpson, a twice-
divorced American, changed the course of British history, as the Duke and Duchess of
Windsor the couple were given the royal treatment during their annual visits to Palm
Beach. Photo Bert Morgan Collection. *State Archives of Florida, Florida Memory.*

Above. In 1968 *Palm Beach Post* society columnist Myrna O'Dell became the fourth Mrs. Russell Firestone Jr. following Firestone's contentious divorce from his third wife. The couple met when she interviewed him for the newspaper during his divorce proceedings. Six years later, O'Dell and Firestone divorced. *Photo Palm Beach Post Archive.*

Above. Many of Midtown's charming bungalows and cottages were supplanted by multi-story apartment houses when Palm Beach was consumed with being modern. *Augustus Mayhew Photography*

11

CHANGES IN ALTITUDE:
HIGH-RISE BOOM

Palm Beach is a one-of-a-kind small town where the bigger the better has been the prevailing standard since Henry Flagler's Royal Poinciana Hotel, once known as the world's largest wood-frame building, transformed the down-to-earth settlement from an unpretentious refuge to an international resort. Whether permitting a ninety-room Addison Mizner-designed oceanfront villa, introducing multi-story office buildings along Royal Palm Way, or attaching a ten-story hotel tower to Whitehall, Palm Beach's building history is exemplified by the demise of the old and the subdued and the rise of the new and the overshadowing.

Despite the lingering sentiment for the 1920s Boom as the town's definitive era, the post-World War II construction frenzy surpassed the barrel-tile-and-stucco mania in dollar value and production volume. The town's upwardly mobile stretch extended from the construction of The Colony and The Ambassador hotels in 1946 until the Town Council imposed new zoning laws in 1970. The laws did away with eight-story, ninety-foot heights and restricted apartments and offices to no more than sixty-foot, five-story buildings.

Although South End or Midtown towers never reached the altitude of the twelve-story Alba-Biltmore Hotel or the high life of nearby Singer Island, their quantity and size impacted Palm Beach's image as an exclusive destination. At the same time buildings were lifting the town skyline far beyond its church steeples, several significant ocean-to-lake estates were being carved into single family subdivisions accommodating smaller houses with modern conveniences. Streetscapes that gave the town its seasonal resort allure linking it with Newport and Bar Harbor were rapidly disappearing.

The shift in aesthetics and economics resulted in Palm Beach attracting a more diverse spectrum of permanent taxpayers rather than tourists seeking sunshine and souvenirs. Cooperative apartment owners, and later condominium residents, were interested in parking garages — not postcards.

South End soars

While South Florida's seasonal storms are frequently remembered for their human toll and ferocity, the hurricane of 1947, however devastating, resulted in a windfall for South End developers. By relocating State Road A1A along the waterway from Manalapan's Vanderbilt Curve to Palm Beach's Sloan's Curve and engineering lakefront landfills on the west side of A1A, the storm's aftermath resulted in twice the number of apartment buildings.

When Cleveland developer Charles Bernstein, along with his brother-in-law Harold Weinstock and nephew Sander "Sandy" Weinstock, began building The Ambassador Hotel on A1A south of Sloan's Curve, the scenic road ran directly along the oceanfront. Following the 1947 storm, the road's realignment along the lake multiplied the Cleveland Shaker Co.'s development potential. During the next decade, under the aegis of Sandy Weinstock, the Ambassador complex was able to add oceanfront and lakefront villas and multi-story apartment buildings.

"I designed the Ambassador apartment buildings along the ocean and lake for Sandy Weinstock," said architect Gene Lawrence. "We were better received by the marketplace than by the town. The town was not too excited. But, since we were within the codes, approvals were never withheld."

Along the oceanfront, Weinstock and Jack Meyerhoff of Baltimore, chairman of the Rouse Co., hired Lawrence to design an eight-story, ninety-six-unit building, with units priced in the $16,000 to $25,000 range. At Ambassador Lakes South, now called the Regency, the lakefront co-op apartments were priced at $30,500. The amenities included soundproof

Above. Built during the post-World War II construction boom, The Colony Hotel's presence towered over nearby Worth Avenue. *Augustus Mayhew Photography.*

Below. Before multi-story condominiums like the Brazilian of Palm Beach were built during the 1960s, Midtown was made up of small hotels, inns and guest houses where tourists rented rooms for the night, the week, or the entire season. *Augustus Mayhew Photography.*

Above. Worth Avenue's Riviera Apartment building was one of several Modernist styled buildings designed by architect John Stetson. *Augustus Mayhew Photography*.

walls and use of The Ambassador Hotel's oceanfront cabanas, pool and dining areas. For this development, Lawrence also designed the molds for the 22,000 decorative blocks used as balcony railings and solar wall screens.

Weinstock, however, was not the only developer to take advantage of the town's broadminded zoning code. He was soon joined by others who saw Palm Beach as a metropolis for the many rather than a seaside enclave for the few.

Unusual marketing edge

In April 1961, New Era Development announced the construction of the Palm Worth, located to the north of the Lake Worth Casino. Designed by architect Edgar Wortman, the five-story oceanfront building's sixty-eight units were sold pre-construction at $16,900 to $32,900. Opened in 1962, the Palm Worth sought a marketing edge over its competitors when it advertised residents would have exclusive use of an on-premise air-raid and fallout shelter.

Not to be outdone, that same year developer Morris Calig and his two sons, Harold and Sam, announced plans for the lakefront President of Palm Beach Hotel. The Caligs offered their guests the First Lady Beauty Salon, managed by a hairstylist named Jacqueline. Built for $1.5 million, the President's crescent-shaped ninety-seven units were designed by West Palm Beach architect Norman Robeson. It offered seasonal residents full hotel service until 1970 when it converted into a condominium with units priced at $16,000 to $43,000. Keeping with Palm Beach's presidential fervor during the Kennedy administration, developers Milton Steinhardt and Louis Mandel built the Palm Beach Whitehouse just south of the Par Three Golf Course. The five-story, fifty-unit building was designed by architect Gilbert Fine. In describing Palm Beach's ever-climbing skyline during this period, a *New York Times* headline read, "National Trend Toward Apartments Evident in Gold Coast resort."

Midtown upturn

Soon after The Colony Hotel opened, architect John Stetson was at work designing the Riviera Apartments at the west end of Worth Avenue. These in-town modern apartments were built featuring a switchboard and maid service, comforts not found in surrounding bungalows and cottages. Later, the eleven-acre lakefront site of the Royal Poinciana Hotel was readied for what was described as the largest apartment hotel building in Florida and the largest poured concrete building of its type in the world.

The Palm Beach Towers' projected construction cost of $8.5 million made for the largest building permit in the town's history. Developers Joseph Mass and Alfred N. Miller retained Washington, D.C. architect John Hans Graham to design the H-shaped multi-story complex's diverse array of more than two-hundred-and-seventy apartments, twenty shops and restaurants.

Formally opened in December 1956, the Palm Beach Towers quickly changed its format from a hotel to an apartment-hotel facility. With the addition of its expanded New Royal Poinciana Room and Regency Room designed by architect Herbert Mathes, the facility was capable of hosting large conventions, banquets and receptions with more than a thousand guests. To the north of this intense development, a suburban-style shopping mall was added. The Royal Poinciana Plaza's shops with large display windows and surrounding asphalt parking lot made for one of Palm Beach's most anomalous commercial developments.

Further changes occurred along the town's scenic lakefront between Worth Avenue and Royal Palm Way when apartment buildings were approved at Nos. 315, 369 and 389 South Lake Drive. Among the most noticeable of the fifteen residential buildings in Midtown designed by architect Howard Chilton, this ensemble of lakefront modernist designs made for a clear-cut distinction between old and new Palm Beach. Nearby, high-rise development continued with Florida Capital Corp.'s six-story $570,000 office building on Royal Palm Way. To the east, the demolition of the Mizner-designed La Fontana and the permitting of the One Royal Palm Way condominium further intensified residents' concern that urbanization threatened Palm Beach's "worldwide image of refined elegance."

On Midtown's oceanfront, the Four-Hundred Building opened as rental apartments. To the north, a $2 million building permit was issued for the construction of the seven-story Ocean Towers complex. At Bradley Place on the North Lake Trail, Louis Pergament retained New York architect Salvatore Bevelacqua to design the eighty-unit Royal Poinciana apartments, with six penthouses.

Above. Built during the mid-1950s, the Palm Beach Towers apartment-hotel was considered the state's largest residential development. *Augustus Mayhew Photography.*

Above. In Midtown, the considerable disparity in altitude between generations is illustrated by The Three Hundred Building co-op built next to an Addison Mizner-designed oceanfront mansion. Following years of litigation, the owners of Mizner's La Fontana were able to demolish it to make way for the One Royal Palm Way condominium. *300 Building collection*.

Below. 300 South Ocean Boulevard, south and west elevations. Designed by Howard Chilton, the co-op apartment building is located across from the Midtown beach. *Augustus Mayhew Photography*.

Concrete in the sunshine

During the mid-1960s, developer Milton Hoff conceived a plan to transform Palm Beach into the Biarritz of Florida. He began by changing the name of his one-hundred-fifty-room Mayflower Hotel to the Palm Beach Spa. Initially built during the 1920s Boom as the Royal Daneli, Hoff promised the hotel would become "the most modern in the world." That is, once he gained approval to add eighty-seven villas and cabanas on the adjacent lot along North Lake Trail. Thus, in May 1965, bulldozers pounded to rubble the fifty-four unit Beaux Arts apartments. Built in 1917, the apartments were a revamp of the once-prized Beaux Arts shopping promenade and movie theater. "I know of no other landmark so steeped in tradition as these buildings," lamented then-Mayor Claude Reese. Nonetheless, the property owner declared the Beaux-Arts had "… fallen victim to progress." Once the Palm Beach Spa facility was completed, Hoff sold the complex to John D. MacArthur.

At the same time McArthur took possession of the Palm Beach Spa, builder Jack Resnick was completing The Sun and Surf between Sunrise and Sunset avenues, replacing the private Sun and Surf Beach Club with what were acknowledged as the town's most expensive rental apartments. Built for $14 million and designed by architect Gene Lawrence, the two-hundred forty-two-unit complex with front door ocean bathing was composed of two modernistic curvilinear seven story buildings housing three restaurants, a beauty salon, exercise rooms, and a barber shop.

In March 1969, Resnick hosted a cocktail party to preview the model apartments with interiors by Park Avenue designer Marilyn Motto. Dubbed a "Historical Party," the event gave the town's local VIPs the last opportunity to recall the personalities who lived in the buildings that were demolished to make room for the Sun and Surf. The *Palm Beach Daily News* described the forthcoming multi-faceted development as "A reflection of the past, luxury of the present and promise of the very near future subtly combined …"

Keeping Palm Beach for the Palm Beachers

In response to the decades of high-rise residential and commercial development, the town's 1969 and 1970 council elections proved revolutionary. While it had always been considered impolite to challenge incumbents, George Mathews won a council seat opposing nine-term

Councilman John Cushman. The following year, with as many as twelve buildings planned for South Ocean Boulevard, Robert Grace and Yvelene "Deedy" Marix were elected. Their incumbent opponents had appeared lax in protecting the town against development.

"The high-rise explosion threatens to destroy the town's unique character," Grace said. "Palm Beach is a worldwide synonym for beauty, quality and value," Marix declared. Matthews, Grace and Marix kept their pledge to scale Palm Beach back to sea level. They immediately tightened building codes and zoning restrictions to reduce the town's population density. At public hearings, residents referred to Palm Beach as "a historic shrine like Newport and Williamsburg."

By March 1970, the town had curbed high-rises, setting a five-story limit on apartments and three-story commercial usage. Church steeples and flagpoles were limited to the same height as the zoning districts in which they are located. Single-family houses were divided into three different types. That summer, the council created an Architectural Commission. Charged with the task to "preserve Palm Beach's beauty," the five-member board of professionals would meet regularly to review building plans. While the town took more than twenty years to restrain its sky's the limit building swell, yet another decade would pass before the Landmarks Preservation Commission was formed.

Today, as Palm Beach contemplates its twenty-first century developments, it might be time to revisit what architects John Stetson and Howard Chilton observed fifty-two years ago in an essay they wrote: "So many times in our attempt to maintain Palm Beach's beauty, we have passed ordinances that prevent duplicating the types of buildings that made the resort famous."

Above. Royal Park's cottages and bungalows were dwarfed by post-World War II co-ops and condominiums built along South Lake Drive. *Historical Society of Palm Beach County.*

Below. Built in 1961 by Modernist architect Howard Chilton, the six-story Southlake condominium overlooks the Town Docks. *Augustus Mayhew Photography*

AUGUSTUS MAYHEW

Augustus Mayhew was born in Cuba, grew up in Delray Beach, and received a bachelor's degree in English Literature and History from Florida State University, having also studied at the university's International Study Center in Florence, Italy. A cultural columnist, architectural historian and photographer, his essays and photographs appear regularly at the New York Social Diary. As a historic preservation activist affiliated with local, regional and state historic preservation organizations, he was the recipient of the AIA-Palm Beach chapter's Historic Preservation Award. The first chairman of Delray Beach's Historic Preservation Board, he was the principal author of the town's preservation ordinance that became a model for the Florida Trust for Historic Preservation. Vice-chairman of Palm Beach County's Historic Resources Review Board, he co-chaired the committee that wrote and implemented the county's historic preservation ad valorem tax exemption ordinance. A former chairman of archives and collections at the Historical Society of Palm Beach County, he is the author of *Lost in Wonderland: Reflections on Palm Beach*.

CPSIA information can be obtained at www.ICGtesting.com
Printed in the USA
LVOW09s1300290416

485942LV00016B/233/P